A COMMENTARY ON ST. PAUL'S SECOND EPISTLE TO THE THESSALONIANS

A COMMENTARY ON ST. PAUL'S SECOND EPISTLE TO THE THESSALONIANS

By the Rev.
ALFRED PLUMMER, M.A., D.D.
Formerly Master of University College, Durham, and sometime Fellow and Tutor of Trinity College, Oxford
Author of "An Exegetical Commentary on the Gospel according to St. Matthew," etc.

Ergo latet ultimus dies,
ut observentur omnes dies.
St. Augustine.

Wipf and Stock Publishers
150 West Broadway • Eugene OR 97401
2001

A Commentary on St. Paul's Second Epistle to the

By Plummer, Alfred

ISBN: 1-57910-666-8

Reprinted by *Wipf and Stock Publishers*
150 West Broadway • Eugene OR 97401

Previously published by London: Robert Scott
, 1918.

INTRODUCTION

I. THESSALONICA

UNDER its modern name of Salonika, Thessalonica, owing to the great war, has become far more widely known than it was previously. Thousands of persons who had hitherto scarcely heard of such a place, and certainly had very vague ideas as to its geographical position, now know accurately where to find it in the map and are aware of its importance with regard to its pr ncipal surroundings. But beyond this fact of its having become a very important city, both from a military and from a political point of view, we are in no better position for understanding the condition of the place at the time when a portion of its inhabitants were a community of the deepest interest to St. Paul and multitudes of other Christians. Nor are we likely to be in a better position for so doing when the war is over. On the contrary, we shall probably find that some of the features which a few years ago were not so very different from what they may have been in his day have been either entirely obliterated or very seriously transformed and disfigured. It is true that the war has added rather considerably to our knowledge of the archaeology of the immediate neighbourhood. Some of those who have been obliged through recent events to take up their abode there for a time have used this opportunity for making explorations in the interests of antiquarian research; and their labours have had considerable results. We are now learning a good deal more about the early history of this interesting tract of country.

But it is about the doings of a people who lived there thousands of years before the coming of St. Paul. Barrows and tombs are being discovered and excavated; but they tell of a race whose existence had been forgotten before the beginning of the Christian era. They throw no light whatever on these earliest Christian writings, produced by missionaries who had come from centres of Eastern civilization, the best elements of which were to be found in Judaism, to preach the Gospel in centres of Western civilization, the best elements of which were to be found in Greek art and literature, and in Roman organization and law.

The missionaries, Paul, Silvanus, and Timothy, had probably planned to begin their enterprise at Philippi; at any rate they did so, and it had obvious advantages. It was a Roman colony and its inhabitants, like Paul and Silvanus, were Roman citizens. It was on the Via Egnatia, the high road between East and West. And although it did not possess a synagogue in which the missionaries could preach, yet it had a settlement of Jews, and a fixed 'place of prayer' by the river Gangites, and there the missionaries could begin. Their success provoked violent opposition and outrageous treatment from the mob and the praetors of Philippi, and the missionaries followed the Lord's counsel (Mt. x. 23) and example (Mt. xii. 15; Mk. iii. 7-12; Jn. x. 39) and went along the great Egnatian road to Thessalonica. Here they were at a seaport, which was a great commercial centre, with a large settlement of Jews and a synagogue. The details of their work there are sufficiently explained in the commentary on the First Epistle to the Thessalonians. Only an outline of it need be given here in order to understand the meaning of the Second Epistle. See Lightfoot, *Biblical Essays*, pp. 237 ff., 253 ff.

In the course of a few weeks of work in the synagogue a few Jews were converted, many 'God-fearers' (religious heathen who attended the synagogue),* and a number of

* See Case, *The Evolution of Early Christianity*, p. 174; Lake, *The Earlier Epp. of St. Paul.* pp. 37 ff.,; Schürer, *Gesch. d. Jüd. Volkes*, III. pp. 123 ff., 3 Auflage. Cf. Zech. viii. 23.

women belonging to the upper classes (Acts xvii. 4). After that, the work took a wider range, and a considerable number of heathen were converted, and this work probably occupied several months (see notes on 1 Thess. i. 9, ii. 9, iii. 12). At the end of it the large majority of the converts were Gentiles. The unconverted Jews were furious at this success among their own people, among the 'God-fearers,' who might otherwise have become Jewish proselytes, and among heathen, whom the Jews had been unable to influence. They stirred up the heathen mob to denounce the missionaries to the Politarchs as preachers of rebellion against Caesar: the missionaries said that there was a Messiah-King coming to found a new Kingdom. The friends of the missionaries advised them to withdraw, and they went to Beroea. Here again all went well at first, till fanatical Jews came from Thessalonica and caused trouble. Friends again advised withdrawal and escorted the Apostle to Athens, leaving Silvanus and Timothy behind. They rejoined him at Athens, and thence Timothy returned to Thessalonica to learn all that he could and report to St. Paul, who meanwhile went on to Corinth, which at that period was socially, politically, and commercially the leading city in Greece. Here all three missionaries were once more united, and the First Epistle to the Thessalonians was written and sent. It had two objects; primarily to answer charges and insinuations which had been urged against the missionaries by their bitter opponents in Thessalonica; and secondly to encourage the converts to persevere and make progress in the Christian life and to give them further instruction in Christian doctrine. Before we consider the occasion and purpose of the Second Epistle, it is necessary to say something about its authenticity, with regard to which doubts are still entertained by scholars whose opinions are of weight.

II. AUTHENTICITY

Extreme views in both directions have been stated with regard to this subject. Some forty years ago, when the Pauline authorship of this Epistle was widely disputed and denied, it was said that "the genuineness of this Letter, like that of the First, is practically uncontroverted" (*N.T. Commentary for English Readers by Various Writers.* Edited by C. J. Ellicott, D.D. Cassels, n.d.). Even at the present time, when doubts and denials are very much less general, that would be a rather exaggerated statement. On the other hand, so lately as 1912, Schweitzer declared that "the Pastoral Epistles and the Second Letter to the Thessalonians profess to be written by the Apostle, but contain not a single thought which is characteristic of his teaching" (*Paul and his Interpreters*, p. 80). That is a more surprising statement than the other. One of the objections brought against the Epistle is that it is too Pauline and looks like the laboured production of an imitator. In these notes passages are pointed out which are thoroughly characteristic of the Apostle's teaching and manner of expressing himself: and, although there are some things for which parallels cannot be found in the other Epistles, yet there is nothing which can be shown to be contradictiory of what is found there. Between 1 and 2 Thessalonians "there is only one very obvious difference, viz., 2 Thess. is far inferior to 1 Thess. in freshness of emotion, in vividness of language, and the winsome expression of friendly fellow-feeling" (Zahn, *Introd. to N.T.*, I. p. 244). This very obvious difference is a strong mark of authenticity. The Apostle is no longer under the influence of the intense feeling of relief and joy, excited by the 'glad tidings' of his converts' 'faith and love' which Timothy had brought back from Thessalonica (1 Thess. iii. 6). On the contrary, he had been hearing of serious misbelief and misconduct (2 Thess. ii. 2, iii. 11), and it was necessary to write in terms of less warm satisfaction and affection, and of increased authority and sternness.

The objections which have been urged against 2 Thess. are modern. Till the end of the 18th century its genuineness was undisputed; but, since Schmidt began the attack in 1801, objections have been frequently urged; and, although of late years objectors have greatly diminished in number and influence, they still exist and are listened to with respect. Some of the objections have been shown to be baseless or trivial, and they ought not to be urged any longer. But this is not the case with all of them. Some are real difficulties which cannot be solved with absolute certainty; suggestions as to possibilities are supplied in the notes. The best general answer to the sum total of the objections lies in this very substantial fact;—the theory that the Epistle is genuine presents far less serious difficulties than the theory that it is not.

As regards *external* evidence the second letter is in a better position than the first. The evidence of the second century begins earlier and it is larger in amount. It begins with Polycarp (*c.* A.D. 115), in whose letter (xi. 3, 4) we seem to have clear references to 2 Thess. i. 4 and iii. 15. Possibly Ignatius (*Rom.* x. 3) shows acquaintance with 2 Thess. iii. 5. More certainly Justin Martyr (*Try.* 110) shows knowledge of 2 Thess. ii. 3. The Epistle is included in the canon of the Syriac, of the Old Latin, of the Muratorian Fragment, and of Marcion. Irenaeus and other writers at the close of the second century quote it by name, and thenceforward it is universally accepted as by St. Paul.

The *internal* evidence is less satisfactory. Here, along with much which confirms the traditional view, we are confronted with difficulties which are more serious than those which have caused hesitation respecting the authenticity of the earlier letter. Even when allowed their full cumulative effect, they leave a decided balance in favour of Apostolic origin. They are sometimes exaggerated, but they are not all unreal. The answers to them are adequate, but they cannot in all cases be regarded as disproof. These objections are based mainly on four things; (1) the language and style, (2) the resemblance, both in arrangement and in wording, to much of the First Epistle, (3) the teaching respecting the Last Things, and (4) the warning against spurious letters, combined with emphatic claim to authenticity (ii. 2, iii. 17).

(1) It is often admitted now that arguments based upon *vocabulary*, and even on *phraseology*, have been over-estimated: in some cases they prove very little. Jülicher, whose discussion of the genuineness of 2 Thess. is admirable, says that in this case the arguments based on the phraseology are the least important, "for on the whole the style is so thoroughly Pauline that one might indeed admire the forger who could imitate it so ingeniously" (*Introd. to N.T.*, p. 62). Reuss says that "the difference between 1 and 2 Cor. is greater than the difference between 1 and 2 Thess. For every 'unpauline' expression the concordance shows ten Pauline, and no single Epistle has so few ἅπαξ λεγόμενα" (*Hist. of N.T.*, p. 75). The occasional expressions for which parallels cannot be found in other Epistles must not, on that account, be regarded as expressions which the Apostle could not have used. "The evidence of style and vocabulary is found to present no insuperable difficulty" (Moffatt, *Lit. of the N.T.*, p. 81.) Suggestions that St. Paul may have given general directions as to what was to be said, and may have left the exact composition to Timothy, or (more probably) to Silvanus, are worthy of consideration; but they are not required.

(2) This second objection is closely connected with the first. On the whole, the *resemblances of 2 Thess. to 1 Thess.* tell more in favour of authenticity than of spuriousness. They may look like imitations by a forger; but they look more like utterances from a man sending a second letter on much the same subjects soon after an earlier letter, and remembering, to a considerable extent, language which he had previously used. That St. Paul had a rough copy of 1 Thess. is not an improbable hypothesis. "Cicero usually treated his letters in this way. Busy as Paul was, and knowing as he did his emotional temperament, nothing was more natural in the circumstances than for him to read over

again the original copy of 1 Thess., if he had it, before dictating 2 Thess." (Zahn, *Introd. to N.T.*, I., p. 250). But the resemblances, which affect only about one-third of 2 Thess., are natural enough, if we regard them as simply the result of memory. They are not greater than those which occur between Ephesians and Colossians, or between 1 and 2 Timothy, or between modern letters written after a brief interval to the same person on the same subjects.*

(3) It is urged that the *eschatology* of 2 Thess. is in general un-Pauline, and is in particular at variance with that of 1 Thess.; also that ii. 3–12 exhibits the ideas of a speculator, who wished to have the authority of the Apostle for these ideas, and who, with 1 Thess. before him, rather clumsily composed this letter in support of them. To this one replies that 2 Thess. ii. 3–12 is *not* at variance with 1 Thess.—1 Thess. says that the Lord will come suddenly; and it implies that He may come very soon, for all are to be ever on the watch. 2 Thess. says that the Day of the Return has not yet dawned, that great events must happen first, and that these events are evidently very near (ii. 7); therefore 2 Thess., like 1 Thess., implies that the Lord may come very soon. It is true that the later Epistle contains details which are not in the earlier one; but there is nothing un-Pauline in them. Baur himself admits that St. Paul might express ideas about Antichrist such as the Jews of his day derived from the prophecies of Daniel, and that such expressions, though they go beyond, do not contradict, the more reserved statements in 1 Cor. xv. 23–28, 51, 52. He also admits that the same writer, full of the thought of the Return, as both 1 and 2 Thess. show, might, at different moments, express himself in different ways (*Life and Work*

* "Apart from the formal agreements in the main epistolary outline, the striking thing is not the slavish dependence of the author of II on I, but the freedom with which he employs the reminiscences from I and incorporates them in original ways into new settings" (Frame, *Thessalonians*, p. 47). See also J. V. Bartlet, *The Apostolic Age*, p. 111.

of Paul, II. pp. 90, 93). These admissions leave little substance in this third objection. In 2 Thess. ii. 3–12 the Apostle, like Christ Himself, is adapting stereotyped Jewish material (which may possibly have absorbed Babylonian elements, as Gunkel supposes) to the purposes of his own teaching. "The 'little apocalypse,' 2 Thess. ii. 3–12, is un-Pauline in precisely the same way that the 'little apocalypse' of Mt. xxiv. and parallels is un-Christian" (B. W. Bacon, *Introd. to N.T.*, p. 77). Both of them, in the mode of their presentation, are Jewish. See also Swete, *Revelation*, pp. lxxv. f., and Briggs, *The Messiah of the Apostles*, p. 84. The Second Epistle contradicts a *misapprehension* of the eschatology of the First, but it does not contradict the eschatology of the First.

(4) It is urged that 2 Thess. ii. 2 implies the existence of a forged letter, and that it is most improbable that any one would, in the Apostle's lifetime, forge a letter in his name to a Church with which he was in such intimate relations; and that iii. 17 is a forger's device to ward off suspicions as to his own production. Here again the objectors' premises are faulty. All that ii. 2 can be supposed to imply is that St. Paul *suspected* the *possibility* of a forgery. Mischievous teachers had assured the Thessalonians that the Apostle had stated that the Day of the Lord had come. He knew that he had never said so either by word or by letter. Was it possible that a letter had been forged? * It is by no means certain that ii. 2 implies even as much as this suspicion; but that is the very most that it implies. Improbable as such a forgery was, it was a possible explanation of the mischievous teaching. With regard to iii. 17, the precaution is much more natural as originating with the Apostle himself, as the notes on the passage indicate. The improbability of forgery either during the Apostle's lifetime or soon after his death adds considerably to our security for the genuineness of 2 Thess. Some of those who still dispute it see that it cannot be placed later than A.D. 70, and

* Lightfoot, *Biblical Essays*, p. 266.

they give A.D. 68–70 as the date of its composition. It is unlikely that any Christian, with whatever innocent motives, would have adopted such a device so very soon after the martyrdom of the Apostle. See Cohu, *S. Paul in the Light of Recent Research,* p. 119.

In discussing the authenticity of 1 Thess., which is now almost universally admitted, it seemed to be sufficient to name twenty scholars, especially such as are not likely to have been prejudiced in favour of traditional views, among the many who accept it. In the case of 2 Thess., which has been much more vigorously assailed, and about which doubts, which cannot be condemned as unreasonable, still exist, it may be worth while to give a longer, though by no means a complete list of the scholars who have come to the conclusion that the Early Church was justified in its universal acceptance of this Epistle as a genuine work of St. Paul. The following British and American scholars adopt this view; Adeney, Alexander, Allen and Grensted, Alford, Askwith, Bacon, Bartlet, Beet, Briggs, Charles, Chase, Conybeare and Howson, Ll. Davies, Denney, Dods, Drummond, Eadie, Ellicott, Farrar, Findlay, Frame, Garrod, Headlam, Jowett, H. H. A. Kennedy, Knowling, K. Lake, Lightfoot, Lillie, Lock, Mason, Milligan, Peake, Salmon, Salmond, Sanday, Schaff, Swete, Vincent. The following continental scholars do the same; Bleek, Börnemann, Brünig, Clemen, Credner, Dobschütz, Döllinger, Ewald, Guericke, J. Grimm, Harnack, Heinrici, Heydenreich, Hofmann, Jacquier, Jülicher, Klöpper, Lueken, Lünemann, Monnet, Nösgen, Reiche, Renan, Reuss, Schäfer, Schott, Vischer, B. Weiss, Wernle, Westrik, de Wette, Wohlenberg, Zahn, Zoechler. Those who care to examine the matter in detail for themselves will probably find that, whatever difficulty they may experience in attributing the Epistle to the Apostle, they will experience greater difficulty in attributing it to any one else. See notes on i. 1, 3, ii. 2, 12, 14, 17, iii. 6, 13, 15, 17.

III. PLACE AND DATE

The place is undoubtedly Corinth, where Silvanus and Timothy rejoined him, after his not very fruitful visit to Athens, and where he stayed for about a year and a half (Acts xvii. 15, xviii. 1, 5, 11). It was in the earlier half of this period that he wrote the First Epistle to the Thessalonians; and the Second was sent not long afterwards,—perhaps only two months later, and probably not more than six. The existing evidence does not admit of exact dating. Chronologers do not agree as to the dates for the leading events in the life of St. Paul, and most of them allow uncertainty as to the date of this Epistle. Harnack says A.D. 48–50; Turner, 50–52; Ramsay, 51–53; Lightfoot and Wiesler, 52–53; Milligan, 50–51; Lewin, 52. Perhaps A.D. 51 is the most probable date. That the eschatology is partly based on the Book of Revelation, and that therefore it was written in the second century, is a view which is perhaps no longer maintained by any one. Even if it were spurious, A.D. 70 would be the limit. Holtzmann, after reciting various arguments for dating 2 Thess. as subsequent to Revelation, says "But to-day the question is not, whether the letter is to be pushed down into the post-apostolic period, but, whether it does not, on the contrary, reach back into the lifetime of the Apostle, and therefore must be genuine" (*Einleitung in d. N.T.*, p. 216).

IV. INTEGRITY.

Closely connected with the questions of authenticity and date is the question of the integrity of the Epistle. It may safely be asserted that, whether genuine or spurious, the whole of it was written at one and the same time. We cannot admit the probability of interpolation. The letter is consecutive and natural in arrangement and has no suspicious breaks. That ii. 1–12 is a later insertion in an otherwise Pauline letter, or (conversely) that it is the only Pauline portion, round which a forger has constructed the rest of the letter, are conjectures which have neither probability nor helpfulness to recommend them. The eschatological portion of ch. i. cannot be separated from the similar portion in ch. ii., as is pointed out in the notes. Still less probable is the hypothesis that i. 5–10, with ii. 1–12, and some portions of iii., belong to a Jewish apocalypse, which a Christian named Paul, but not the Apostle, put together in a Christian form with additions of his own. None of these reconstructions has the smallest support from MSS., or Versions, or quotations in the Fathers; nor does any one of them commend itself by its intrinsic merit. They do not repay serious examination.

V. OCCASION

The reasons for sending the Second Epistle can be gathered from the Epistle itself. It is probable that the person who carried the First Epistle to Thessalonica returned soon afterwards and reported to St. Paul and his colleagues as to the condition of the Thessalonian converts; and it is possible that he brought with him a letter from the Thessalonians, although there is very small evidence of this in the second letter to them (see on i. 3, 11, iii. 3). It is possible also that travellers from Thessalonica to Corinth brought information. It is certain that in some way or other information did reach the Apostle and his companions (iii. 11). It was of a mixed character. On the one hand, the converts were enduring bitter persecution and affliction with great fortitude, and were growing in brotherly love towards one another (i. 3, 4). On the other hand, there had been serious misapprehension, if not deliberate misrepresentation, of the Apostle's teaching respecting the Second Advent (ii. 2, 3), and it was necessary to correct this. Moreover the brief warning against disorderly conduct (1 Thess. v. 14) had had little or no effect; the evil had seriously increased, and it was necessary to give strict injunctions with a view to putting a stop to it. These are the circumstances which occasioned the Second Epistle, and they amply explain its character. The Apostle gives generous praise to what is satisfactory, makes clear his actual teaching about the Second Advent, and with conscious authority deals firmly, but not harshly, with the prevalent excitement and idleness.

VI. CONTENTS

(*a*) The letter follows the lines of letter-writing which were usual at that period, and the topics follow in a natural order, which to some extent may have been arranged beforehand.* There are three main divisions, one in each of the three chapters. These divisions are preceded by the usual Salutation and are followed by the usual Salutation and Benediction.

I. The Salutation, i. 1, 2.

II. Historical and Doctrinal. *Thanksgiving, Doctrine, and Prayer*, i. 3–12.

1. Thanksgiving for the Converts' Stedfastness and Progress, i. 3–4.
2. Doctrine of the Righteousness of God's Judgments, i. 5–10.
3. Prayer for the Thessalonian Christians, i. 11, 12.

III. Doctrinal and Hortatory. *Doctrine, Thanksgiving and Exhortation, and Prayer*, ii. 1–17.

1. Doctrine concerning the Time of the Lord's Coming, and the Revelation of the Lawless One, ii. 1–12.

* "These two letters (1 and 2 Thess.) are hardly equalled even by those to the Galatians and Corinthians, in that direct, easy, conversational manner which is the peculiar quality of a genuine letter, marking it off from the studied epistles" (Vernon Bartlet).

2. Thanksgiving and Exhortation, ii. 13–15.
3. Prayer for the Thessalonian Christians, ii. 16, 17.

IV. Cheering and Commanding. *Request, Encouragement, Reproofs, Instruction, and Prayers,* iii. 1–16.

1. Request, Encouragement and Prayer, iii. 1–5.
2. Reproofs and Instructions, iii. 6–15.
3. Prayer for the Thessalonian Christians, iii. 16.

V. Concluding Salutation and Benediction, iii. 17, 18.

(*b*) *Reminiscences of the Septuagint.*

St. Paul's familiarity with the language of the LXX is less conspicuous in this letter than in the earlier, not merely because this letter is shorter (47 verses against 89), but because the substance of it has less resemblance to passages in the O.T. As in the First Epistle, there are no direct quotations ; but there are a few in which he certainly had passages in the LXX in his mind, and one or two more in which he may have done so. These are almost entirely confined to the two portions of his apocalypse, the introduction in i. 6–12, and the main portion in ii. 3–12. Single words, like ἀνταποδοῦναι (i. 6), do not count for much, but in this case the Septuagint word is quickly followed by language which comes direct from the LXX.

2 *Thessalonians*		*Septuagint*	
i. 7 8.	*ἐν πυρὶ φλογός, διδόντος ἐκδίκησιν τοῖς μὴ εἰδόσι Θεὸν καὶ τοῖς μὴ ὑπακούουσιν.*	Exod. iii. 2.	*ἐν πυρὶ φλογός.*
		Is. lxvi. 15.	*ἀποδοῦναι ἐν θυμῷ ἐκδίκησιν αὐτοῦ καὶ ἀποσκορακισμὸν αὐτοῦ ἐν φλογὶ πυρός.*
		Jer. x. 25.	*ἔκχεον τὸν θυμόν σου ἐπὶ ἔθνη τὰ μὴ εἰδότα σε.*
		Ps. lxxviii. 6	*ἐπὶ ἔθνη τὰ μὴ ἐπεγνωκότα σε.,*

i. 9, 10.	ἀπὸ προσώπου τοῦ Κυρίου καὶ ἀπὸ τῆς δόξης τῆς ἰσχύος αὐτοῦ, ὅταν ἔλθῃ ἐνδοξασθῆναι ἐν τοῖς ἁγίοις αὐτοῦ κ. θαυμασθῆναι ἐν πᾶσιν τοῖς πιστεύσασιν.	Is. ii. 10.	ἀπὸ προσώπου τοῦ φόβου Κυρίου καὶ ἀπὸ τῆς δόξης τῆς ἰσχύος αὐτοῦ, ὅταν ἀναστῇ θραῦσαι τὴν γῆν.
		Ps. lxvii. 36.	θαυμαστὸς ὁ Θεὸς ἐν τοῖς ὁσίοις αὐτοῦ.
		Ps. lxxviii. 8.	ὁ Θεὸς ἐνδοξαζόμενος ἐν βουλῇ ἁγίων.
i. 10	ἐν τῇ ἡμέρᾳ ἐκείνῃ.	Is. ii. 12; Joel iii. 18; Obad. 8; Zech. ii. 11, etc.	
i. 12.	ὅπως ἐνδοξασθῇ τὸ ὄνομα τοῦ Κυρίου.	Is. lxvi. 5.	ἵνα τὸ ὄνομα Κυρίου δοξασθῇ.
ii. 2.	ἡμέρα τοῦ Κυρίου.	Is. ii. 12; Ezek. iii. 5.	ἡμέρα Κυρίου.
ii. 3, 4.	ὁ ἄνθρωπος τ. ἀνομίας ὁ αντικείμενος καὶ ὑπεραιρόμενος ἐπὶ πάντα λεγόμενον θεὸν ἢ σέβασμα ὥστε αὐτὸν εἰς τὸν ναὸν τοῦ Θεοῦ καθίσαι, ἀποδεικνύντα ἑαυτὸν ὅτι ἔστιν Θεός.	Dan. xi. 36, 37.	ποιήσει κατὰ τ. θέλημα αὐτοῦ, καὶ ὑψωθήσεται ἐπὶ πάντα θεόν, καὶ ἐπὶ τ. Θεὸν τ. θεῶν ἔξαλλα λαλήσει, και εὐοδωθήσεται ἕως ἂν συντελεσθῇ ἡ ὀργή· καὶ ἐπὶ τοὺς θεοὺς τῶν πατέρων αὐτοῦ οὐ μὴ προνοηθῇ· ὅτι ἐν παντὶ ὑψωθήσεται. εἰς αὐτὸν γὰρ συντέλεια γίνεται.
ii. 7.	ἕως ἐκ μέσου γένηται.		
ii. 4.	ὁ υἱὸς τῆς ἀπολείας.		
ii. 8.	ὁ ἄνομος.	Ezek. iii. 18, 19, xviii. 21, 24, xxxiii. 8, etc.	

ii. 8.	*ἀνελεῖ τῷ πνεύματι τοῦ στόματος αὐτοῦ.*	Is. xi. 4.	*πατάξει τῷ λόγῳ τοῦ στόματος αὐτοῦ.*
		Job. iv. 9.	*ἀπὸ πνεύματος ὀργῆς αὐτοῦ ἀφανισθήσονται.*
ii. 13.	*ἠγαπημένοι ὑπὸ Κυρίου.*	Deut. xxxiii. 12.	*ἠγαπημένος ὑπὸ τοῦ Κ.*
		Ecclus. xxxv. 1.	*ἠγαπημένος ὑπὸ Θεοῦ.*

Under this head a few words may be said respecting the views which the writers evidently had respecting the relation between Christ and the Father.

As in the First Epistle, the Christology appears only incidentally, and for that reason is all the more decisive. The Father and Christ are placed together as equal in dignity, i. 1, 2, 12, ii. 16. *Κύριος*, which in the LXX represents the ineffable 'Jehovah' or 'Yahve,' is frequently transferred to Christ; see the last note on i. 1. In the apocalyptic passages, i. 7–10, ii. 3–12, imagery which in the O.T. is used of God is transferred without scruple or explanation to Christ. 'The Name of our Lord Jesus' (i. 12) is used in a sense parallel to 'the Name of the Lord' in the O.T. In one of the prayers (ii. 16, 17) Christ is placed before the Father, and the verbs which follow are in the singular. Theodoret (*Ep.* 146) calls attention to this, as "teaching that the order of the Names does not indicate a distinction of dignity and nature." Christ is spoken of as in Heaven, whence He will come in great glory to punish the wicked and reward the good, i. 6, 7, ii. 8, 14.

(*c*) *The Man of Lawlessness or Man of Sin.*

For the purposes of this commentary not much need be added to what is said in the notes respecting this interminable, and (for some persons) very fascinating subject. Those who desire to acquaint themselves with the main views which have been held on the subject can find a great deal of information in the commentaries on 2 *Thessalonians* by Alford, Findlay, Frame, Garrod, Jowett, and Milligan; on the *Epistles of St. John* by Brooke, Law, and Westcott; and on the *Apocalypse of St. John* by Simcox, Swete, and many others. See also articles on 'Antichrist,' 'Man of Sin,' 'False Christs,' and 'Eschatology' in Biblical Dictionaries and Encyclopaedias. In all these places references will be found to other literature on the subject, the amount of which is enormous. A large portion of what has been written may now be treated as obsolete, because in it interpretations are advocated which are generally admitted to be no longer tenable. A very full and searching commentary on the Book of Revelation (*Int. Crit. Comm.*) is now in the Press, and it contains an admirable Additional Note on ch. xvii, of which, through the great kindness of the writer, Canon R. H. Charles, I am allowed to make full use.

After tracing the independent development of the Antichrist, Beliar, and Neronic myths, in which sometimes a God-opposing individual, and sometimes a God-opposing power or "collective Antichrist," is prominent, the writer discusses the fusion of the Antichrist myth with that of Beliar.

"As a result of this fusion the Antichrist is regarded as (*a*) a God-opposing man armed with miraculous powers—this appears to have been effected on Christian soil before 50 A.D.; (*b*) a purely Satanic power before 70 A.D.

"(*a*) 2 Thess. ii. 1–12, according to the usual interpretation, presents an indubitable instance of this fusion. Thus, on the one hand, we have Beliar. 'The man of lawlessness' (ὁ ἄνθρωπος τῆς ἀνομίας) is all but certainly a translation of Beliar; for ἀνόμημα is the LXX rendering of it in Deut. xv. 9, and ἀνομία in 2 Kings [2 Sam.] xxii. 5, and παράνομος is frequently found as its equivalent, when it is used as an epithet: Deut. xiii. 13; Judges xix. 22, xx. 13; 2 Kings [2 Sam.] xvi. 7, etc.

"In the next place it is Beliar appearing as Antichrist; for the words 'he that opposeth himself . . . against all that is called God' form an excellent definition of the Antichrist. Since 2 Thess. is now generally (and certainly by the present writer) regarded as an authentic writing of St. Paul, we have here the earliest evidence for the fusion of these ideas (*circ.* 50 A.D.) and also for *the humanization of the Beliar myth through its fusion with that of the Antichrist*; for hitherto Beliar had been conceived as a Satanic or super-human being. The Antichrist thus comes to be conceived as *a God-opposing man armed with Satanic powers.*

"We should next observe that in 2 Thess. ii. 1–12 the myth appears to have a purely *religious* significance and not a *political* one, as in Rev. xiii. 1–10, xvii. Thus in 2 Thess. ii. 6, 7 the Roman Empire is referred to as the power which checks the manifestation of the Antichrist, whereas in Rev. xiii. 1–10 it is the Roman Empire which stands in the background as the Antichrist, while the demonic Nero stands in the foreground as this being. In no case could 2 Thess. ii. 1–12 have been written after 70 A.D. This section is a Christian transformation of a current Judaistic myth."

To ask, as some are doing, whether St. Paul and St. John, in their pictures of the Antichrist, were predicting the enormities committed by the German Emperor and his people during the present war, is to ask a futile question. The inspired writers were giving instruction, encouragement, and warning to Christians of their own time. What help would it have been to Christians of the first two centuries to have cryptic descriptions of horrors that were to take place in the twentieth century? And how could teachers who were fully persuaded that Christ would return very soon, and bring this world to a close, be supposed to foresee what would be going on in this world many centuries later? What they did see was this;—that any God-opposing power, however successful for a time in making might prevail against right, and however skilful in adapting miracles of science to its own wicked purposes, must in the end fail, and be destroyed by the righteous judgment of God. Moral principles may be derided and reversed. "We ought, therefore we can" may be transformed into "We can, therefore we ought," so that the power to conquer is made to imply the right to conquer: but sooner or later the mills of God accomplish their inevitable work, and the monstrous rebel is ground to powder.

Ὀψὲ Θεοῦ ἀλέουσι μύλοι, ἀλέουσι δὲ λεπτά.

VII. COMMENTARIES

Only a selection is given here. A very full list will be found in the excellent commentary by Professor J. E. Frame, who has had the advantage of coming last in a very distinguished list. In the following summary foreign works which have been translated into English are inserted in the English list.

On the Greek Text.

Patristic.

Greek. Chrysostom, Theodore of Mopsuestia,* Theodoret, Oecumenius.

Latin. Ambrosiaster, Pelagius.

Reformers.

Latin. Calvin, Zwingli, Musculus.

Modern.

Bengel, *Gnomon N.T.*, 1742; tr. 1857, 1860.
Webster and Wilkinson, 1855–1861.
Lillie, 1856 (American).
Alford, 1857, 5th ed. 1871.
Olshausen, 1830; tr. 1858.
Jowett, 1859.
C. Wordsworth, 1859.
Eadie, 1877.
Lüneman, 1850 (in Meyer); tr. 1880.
Ellicott, 1880.
Garrod, 1900.

* See Swete's admirable edition of the Latin Version with the Greek Fragments; also (for information respecting all these writers) his *Patristic Study*, and Hastings' *D.B.* vol V. art 'Patristic Commentaries' by C. H. Turner. Swete's *Theodore* has been often used for the notes in this volume.

Lightfoot, 1895 (Posthumous, in *Notes on the Epistles of St. Paul*).
Findlay, 1904 (*Cambridge Greek Testament*).
B. Weiss, 1902; tr. 1906.
Milligan, 1908.
Moffatt, 1910 (*Expositor's Greek Testament*).
Frame, 1912 (*International Critical Commentary*).

On the English Versions.

Mason (*Ellicott's Com. for English Readers*).
Alexander, 1881 (*Speaker's Commentary*).
Marcus Dods, 1882 (*Schaff's Popular Com.*).
Gloag, 1887 (*Pulpit Commentary*).
Findlay (1891) (*Cambridge Bible*).
Denney, 1892 (*Expositor's Bible*).
Bartlet, 1902 (*Temple Bible*).
Adeney (*New Century Bible*).

New Translations into English.

The Twentieth Century New Testament, 1900.
Weymouth, *The N.T. in Modern Speech,* 1905.
Way, *The Letters of St. Paul,* 2nd. ed. 1906.
Rutherford (Posthumous), *Thessalonians and Corinthians,* 1908.
Moffatt, *The N.T., a New Translation,* 1913.
Cunnington, *The New Covenant,* 1914.

There are valuable articles on the Epistle in Smith's *D.B.* by Lightfoot, 1863; Hastings' *D.B.* by Lock, 1902; Cheyne's *Enc. Bibl.* by McGiffert, 1903; Murray's *Illustrated Bible Dictionary* by Sinker. See also the article on "Paul" in Hastings' *D.C.G.* vol. II., by Sanday.

Of German commentaries those by Schmiedel, 1892 (in Holt mann), Börnemann, 1894 (in Meyer), Zoeckler, 1894, Wohlenberg, 1903 (in Zahn), Lueken, 1908 (in J. Weiss), and Dobschütz, 1909 (in Meyer), will be found useful.

In the quotations from the A.V., *italics* signify that the word is not expressed in the Greek.

In the paraphrase, *italics* signify that the word is emphatic. Paraphrase is necessary, because no mere translation, however accurate, can convey the fulness of the Apostle's meaning to the English reader.

A COMMENTARY ON ST. PAUL'S SECOND EPISTLE TO THE THESSALONIANS

i. 1, 2. THE SALUTATION

i. [1] Paul, and Silvanus, and Timotheus unto the Church of the Thessalonians, in God our Father, and the Lord Jesus Christ: [2] Grace unto you, and peace from God our Father, and the Lord Jesus Christ.

The Salutation in 2 Thessalonians is longer than the Salutation in the First Epistle in two respects; it adds 'our' (ἡμῶν) to 'Father' in *v.* 1, and it adds 'from God the Father and the Lord Jesus Christ' to 'Grace unto you and peace' in *v.* 2. In both respects the addition is in harmony with St. Paul's usage elsewhere. For 'our Father' see 1 Thess. i. 3; 2 Thess. ii. 16; Rom. i. 7; 1 and 2 Cor. i. 2; Eph. i. 2; Phil. i. 2; Col. i. 2; Philem. 2. Here 'our' is wanting in some important authorities, and it has perhaps been inserted because of the usage elsewhere. But the longer addition is certainly genuine here, although not in 1 Thess. i. 1, where it has been inserted in inferior authorities because of its presence in subsequent Epistles. It intimates that the ultimate source of grace and peace is the Father and Jesus Christ. As in all the other Pauline Salutations in which these words occur, the preposition ἐν is not repeated before 'the Lord Jesus Christ,' and thus no distinction is made between the Father and the Saviour, as if one was the source, and the other merely the channel, of the grace and peace. Contrast Jn.

xx. 17, where 'my' and 'your' indicate the difference between Christ and the disciples in their relation to the Father and God. In Col. i. 2 the Father alone is mentioned.

In other respects the Salutation implies a great deal more than at first sight appears, as the following paraphrase shows.

[1] Paul and Silvanus and Timothy, well known to you as friends and instructors, to the Assembly of Thessalonians who [like ourselves] have God as Father and Jesus Christ as Lord, and are thereby united as children in one family and as members in one body : [2] We send you the Christian and the Jewish greeting combined—grace, the source of all spiritual blessings, and peace, the end and issue of them all—desiring that you may receive them from God the Father and the Lord Jesus Christ.

1. In neither of these two Epistles, nor in Philippians, does St. Paul begin by styling himself an Apostle. The reason probably is that neither at Thessalonica nor at Philippi had his authority as an Apostle been questioned. All three letters are written in terms of affection and instruction, rather than of official relation, although the voice of authority is heard where it is needed. The omission of 'Apostle' is a mark of genuineness; an imitator, with a knowledge of St. Paul's usage elsewhere, would be likely to insert it, all the more so with a wish to gain authority for his own production.

Silvanus (1 Thess. i. 1; 2 Cor. i. 19; 1 Pet. v. 12) is the same person as Silas (Acts xv. 22–xviii. 5). Three theories may safely be rejected; (1) that Silas and Silvanus are different persons; (2) that one of the two is to be identified with Titus; (3) that Silas, Silvanus and Titus are names of one and the same person. Silas is probably the Jewish name, of which Silvanus is the Latin equivalent denoting Roman citizenship. The abbreviation of Silvanus would be Silvas rather than Silas. Zahn, *Intr. to the N.T.*, I. p. 31. Silvanus was probably a Hellenistic Jew and a Roman citizen. As one of the 'chief men among the brethren' (Acts xv. 22) and a 'prophet' (xv. 32), and senior both in age and in service, he is placed before Timothy, who was perhaps less known at Thessalonica. He is placed before Timothy Acts xvii. 14. He was entirely in sympathy with St. Paul—more so perhaps than Barnabas, in the desire to convert the Gentiles.

Timothy was probably converted by the Apostle himself during the first journey in Asia Minor; he is conspicuous in all the Pauline Epistles, excepting Galatians, Colossians, and Titus. Cf. Acts. xvi. 1; 1 Cor. xvi. 10; Phil. ii. 20, 22. He is associated with the Apostle in the opening Salutation in Epistles of three groups; 1 and 2 Thess.; 2 Cor.; Phil., Col., Philem. In the fourth group two letters are addressed to him. The A.V. wavers between 'Timotheus' and 'Timothy,' even in the same chapter (2 Cor. i. 9. 19), with a decided preference for 'Timotheus' (Acts, Rom., 1 Cor., Phil., 1 and 2 Thess.); but with 'Timothy' fairly often (1 and 2 Tim., Philem., Heb.).* It is possible that Timothy stayed behind at Philippi for a short time after St. Paul and Silvanus had gone on to Thessalonica; for in Acts (where only the first few weeks of the mission are mentioned) he is not mentioned as being at Thessalonica. It is clear from '*they* departed' (not '*we* departed') in Acts xvi. 40 that *Luke* was left behind at Philippi (contrast 'us' in xvi. 16); but we know from these two letters that, whether left behind at Philippi or not, Timothy certainly did work at Thessalonica with St. Paul and Silvanus. His being the son of a Greek (Acts xvi. 1) may have helped him there.

The 1st person plural is used in both Epistles repeatedly; 1 Thess. i. 2, 5, 6, ii. 4, 8, 13, 18–20; 2 Thess. i. 3, 11, ii. 1, iii. *passim*; and it is probable that this is not the official 'we' of an author, but that it includes Silvanus and Timothy, who had had a large share in the conversion of the Thessalonians, and in establishing the converts as a Christian Church. Nevertheless it is not probable that Silvanus had much share in the production of either letter. But Timothy may have been the scribe to whom 1 Thessalonians was dictated; and it is *possible* that he or Silvanus may have been

* 'Timotheus' is, of course, a word of four syllables, one long and three short. One often hears it read as a world of three long syllables, which entirely obscures the derivation.

allowed to write a good deal of 2 Thessalonians from instructions given him by the Apostle rather than from actual dictation. This, however, is pure conjecture, to explain the similarities and differences between the two Epistles. A. S. Way turns the plurals into singulars throughout, which is arbitary.

to the Assembly of Thessalonians] 'Assembly' rather than 'Church,' because at the time when these letters were written *ecclesia* had hardly become a distinctly Christian term.* Both Jews and Greeks used *ecclesia* to denote their assemblies, and as there were both Jews and Greeks in the Apostolic Church, the Christian use of the term might have come from either. It is probable, however, that the Jewish use of it was the fact which chiefly influenced the Christian use; Hort, *The Christian Ecclesia*; Swete, *The Holy Catholic Church.* In Judith vi. 16 the A.V. has 'assembly,' in Ecclus. xxiv. 2, l. 13, and 1 Macc. ii. 56 'congregation.' In his later Epistles, Romans, Ephesians, Colossians, and Philippians, the Apostle does not address the "assembly" or 'church,' but 'the saints,' *i.e.* the Christians in each place.

In these two early letters the Apostle names the *people*, the Thessalonians, not the *city*, Corinth, Rome, Philippi, Colossae. In Galatians, which may be placed between Thessalonians and Corinthians, he names the *country*, Galatia.

The addition 'in God . . . Jesus Christ' distinguishes the assembly which is addressed from the assemblies of Gentiles and Jews with which the Thessalians were familiar. Gentiles did not recognize God as Father, and neither Gentiles nor Jews recognized Jesus as Lord. This addition is in both 1 and 2 Thessalonians, but in no other Epistle. *Inde colligendum est, non alibi quaerendum esse Ecclesiam, nisi ubi praeest Deus, ubi Christus regnat* (Calvin). Although the heathen are generally ignorant of the fact, all men in their highest aspect are 'in God'; and, although be-

* Tyndale and Cranmer have 'congregation' here.

lievers are often forgetful of the fact, all Christians are 'in Christ.' Rutherford here has 'inherent in.'

In this combination we have at once what is the most marked feature in these two early Epistles,—the equal emphasis on God the Father and the Lord Jesus Christ; cf. ii. 16; 1 Thess. iii. 11. In no Epistle is the Holy Spirit mentioned in the Salutation, whereas the 'Lord Jesus Christ' is specially frequent at the beginning of Pauline and other Epistles. It is unlikely that St. Paul originated it; more probably in this, as in many other expressions, he used language which was already stereotyped. Whoever was the first to employ it, it is very significant that the Greek equivalent of the ineffable 'Jehovah' should be welcomed as a natural title of Jesus Christ. In 1 Thessalonians Christ is called 'the Lord' more than twenty times. In this letter 'the Lord Jesus Christ' occurs again *vv.* 2, 12, iii. 12; 'our Lord Jesus Christ' ii. 2, 14, 16, 18; 'the Lord Jesus' i. 7, ii. 8; 'our Lord Jesus' i. 8, 12. Such expressions are also very common in Philippians. There may be some reason why Christ is so often called 'the Lord' in the letters addressed to the Macedonian Churches.

In the LXX Κύριος is used for Jehovah as well as for Adonai innumerable times. "The change of usage by Paul in applying 'Lord' so exclusively to Christ and in carefully abstaining from using it for God the Father was a radical change of an importance which it is hard for any one to exaggerate. It involved the practical substitution of the sovereignty of the Messiah for the sovereignty of God during the Messianic age" (Briggs, *The Messiah of the Apostles*, pp. 86, 87; see also Zahn, *Introd. to N.T.*, I. p. 254). *Jésus est le Seigneur, le Christ, un personage entièrement surhumain, non Dieu encore, mais bien près de l'être. On vit en lui, on meurt en lui, on ressuscite en lui; presque tout qu'on dit de dieu, on le dit de lui* (Renan, *Saint Paul*, p. 274).

2. We may perhaps say that it is also unlikely that St. Paul was the first to use the combination 'grace and peace.' It is found in 1 and 2 Peter, 2 John, and Revelation; and the fact that it is used by such different writers suggests that the expression was current as a Christian password, whoever may have originated it. See Charles on Rev. i. 4. In the O.T. 'grace' is rare in the Psalms and Prophets, but is frequent in the Wisdom Books. In the N.T. it is found far more often in the Pauline Epistles than in all the other Books together. In the Johannine writings it is rare. From its original meaning of pleasingness and charm in person and address, 'grace' acquired the moral sense of pleasingness in character, 'graciousness'; and when used of God, as so often in Scripture, it expresses God's mercy and favour to mankind. In the N.T. it is specially used of God's favour as manifested in the life and work of His incarnate Son; and this is the meaning that is so common in the Pauline Epistles, especially when combined with 'peace,' as here. The favour of God produces peace of mind, because enmity to God has ceased, and reconciliation with Him has been effected. In conversion from heathenism (which is what had been the case with most of the Thessalonian Christians) the tormenting dread of offending this or that god or goddess or daemon was extinguished. Polytheism is fatal to peace of mind. Every detail of life is supposed to be presided over by some unseen power, who must be propitiated, or it will take vengeance. Moreover, these unseen powers are believed to be jealous of one another; and to sacrifice to the wrong one may be more fatal than neglecting to sacrifice to any. Tatian (*Address to the Greeks*, xxix.) tells of the relief of being rescued from slavery to ten thousand tyrants and taught to worship one benevolent God. T. R. Glover, *The Jesus of History*, p. 206; Renan, *Hibbert Lectures* 1880, p. 11. On the meanings of 'grace' in the N.T. see Sanday and Headlam on Rom. i. 5; J. A. Robinson, Ephesians, pp. 221 f.; Findlay on 1 Thess. i. 1 and 2 Thess. i. 12.

i. 3—12. HISTORICAL AND DOCTRINAL

On the whole, the main divisions of the Epistle correspond to the divisions of the chapters; but the same kinds of subjects are found in more than one of the three divisions, so that it is not easy to give satisfactorily distinctive headings to each. There is Thanksgiving and Doctrine in both the first and the second chapters; there is Exhortation in both the second and the third; and there is Prayer in all three. All three of the main divisions end with prayer for the Thessalonian Christians; and this is one reason for believing that the letter has three main divisions rather than two. The personal element, which is so conspicuous in the First Epistle, is almost entirely absent; in this letter the Apostle says very little about himself.

i. 3-12. THANKSGIVING, DOCTRINE, AND PRAYER

The discovery of vast quantities of papyri has taught us that the Thanksgivings which are such a marked feature in almost all the letters of St. Paul are in accordance with what was customary in the ordinary correspondence of his time. Expressions of gratitude to the gods were common at the beginning of secular letters. Deissmann, *Light from the Ancient East*, p. 169, quotes an interesting example from the 2nd cent. A.D. "Apion to Epimachus his father and lord, many greetings. Before all things I pray that thou art in health, and that thou dost prosper and fare well continually together with my sister and her daughter and my brother. I thank the Lord Serapis that when I was in peril in the sea, he saved me immediately, etc." In the letters of St. Paul, however, the Thanksgivings are no mere followings of customary forms. They serve a serious purpose. They are intended to induce those to whom they are addressed to listen attentively and sympathetically to the contents of the Epistle. The first two verses here (3, 4) are really a commendation of the Thessalonians expressed "in the form of a Thanksgiving on their behalf, in which, as elsewhere, the power of expression falls short of the fulness of his heart" (Jowett). Thus in one sense the Thanksgiving in this Epistle is very brief, for it quickly shades off into Doctrine (5–10), and thence passes into Prayer (11, 12). There is scarcely room for a colon, and none for a full stop, until the end of *v.* 10. Nevertheless, the transitions are so easy that the whole chapter might be regarded as representing the usual Thanksgiving, in which case it is not exceptionally brief, but exceptionally long. The Thanksgiving in Romans is in this respect somewhat similar. As in the long Thanksgiving in 1 Thess. i. 2–10, we have a good example of St. Paul's style, allowing his sentences to grow one out of the other, like shoots from a vine stalk, as thoughts occur to him, instead of keeping them distinct and balanced, as we find them in the Epistle to the Hebrews. For convenience we may divide the remainder of the chapter into the three sections indicated above.

i. 3, 4. Thanksgiving for the Converts' Stedfastness and Progress

The purpose of the Thanksgiving is to encourage the fainthearted by praise of their faith and love and hopeful endurance under persecution.

3 We are bound to thank God always for you, brethren, as it is meet, because that your faith groweth exceedingly, and the charity of every one of you all towards each other aboundeth : 4 So that we ourselves glory in you in the Churches of God, for your patience and faith in all your persecutions and tribulations that ye endure.

In expressing this thankfulness the Apostle seems to have been influenced to a limited extent, either consciously or unconsciously, by what had been said in the earlier letter, especially in the transition (4, 5) from gratitude to God to the thought of a judgment to come. But the two Thanksgivings are in the main quite independent. An imitator, who was using the earlier one as a model, would be likely to produce far more resemblance. The full meaning is in each case impressive.

[3] We continually feel, and cannot help feeling, bound to give thanks to the one and only God on all occasions for you, Brethren, and you have fully deserved this by your conduct ; we feel bound, I say, because your faith in Him and the Lord Jesus Christ continues to increase more and yet more, and because the love which every single individual among you all bears towards every other continues to be more and more widely diffused. You yourselves doubtless rejoice at this. [4] And it has its effect upon *us* also, for it prompts us naturally enough, as being those who planted this faith and love in you, to glory about you in the Christian congregations which God has raised elsewhere, boasting of the strength of endurance and constancy of faith, which has been and is maintained and manifested by you in all the persecutions and the afflictions which you are still enduring for the Gospel's sake.

3. **We continually feel**] St. Paul often says that he does give thanks to God, but only in this letter (i. 3, ii. 13) does he speak of feeling bound to do so ; and the word which he uses about this feeling is one which implies an obligation that binds particular individuals (ὀφείλομεν Rom. xv. 1, 27), as distinct from one that is rooted in the nature of things (δεῖ 1 Cor. xv. 25, 53 ; 2 Cor. v. 10 ; etc.). The word for 'to thank' (εὐχαριστεῖν) meant originally 'to do a good turn to' ; then 'to return a favour' ; and hence 'to express gratitude,' which is its Scriptural meaning. With St. Paul most things are looked at from the point of view of personal duty. Barnabas v. 3 has "we feel bound to be very thankful to the Lord," ὑπερευχαριστεῖν ὀφείλομεν τῷ Κυρίῳ.

'*We* continually feel' not '*I* continually feel.' As already stated, the 1st person plural prevails, and it almost certainly includes Silvanus and Timothy. Contrast 1 Cor. i. 4, where we have 'I thank,' although Sosthenes is coupled with St. Paul in the Salutation ; and Phil. i. 3 and Philem. 4, where we have 'I thank,' although Timothy is coupled with St. Paul in the Salutation. In 2 Cor. i.–ix., as in 1 and 2 Thess., the 1st pers. plur. prevails. The present tense indicates that the feeling of obligation is lasting. Contrast *gratiasque egi, ut debui*, Cic. *Ad Fam.* xiv. 2 ; and compare *merito e vestro maximas vobis gratias omnes et agere et habere debemus,* Cic. *Phil.* iii. 10.

to the one and only God] In the Greek, 'to God' has the article, which may distinguish 'the God' of the Christians from the numerous deities of the heathen.

on all occasions] A stronger expression (πάντοτε) than 'always' (ἀεί). It is late Greek and is equivalent to the classical ἑκάστοτε. In the N.T. it has almost driven ἀεί out of use. See on διὰ παντός iii. 16, and cf. ἐν παντί 1 Thess. v. 18; 2 Cor. iv. 18, vi. 4, vii. 5, 11, etc.

for you, Brethren] Vulg. *pro vobis,* Beza *de vobis.* Cf. *v.* 11, ii. 13, iii. 1. The omission of 'all' and the insertion of 'Brethren' are probably not accidental. 1 Thess i. 2 we have περὶ πάντων ὑμῶν without ἀδελφοί. There are now disorderly persons (iii. 11) among the Thessalonians, whose misconduct is one of the things which have evoked this official and authoritative letter. But the severity of the letter is mitigated by the insertion of 'Brethren' at the beginning of each of the three divisions, as well as elsewhere (ii. 13, 15, iii. 6, 13); yet it is not so frequent as in the earlier and more affectionate letter.

You have fully deserved this] Lit. 'even as it is meet' (καθὼς ἄξιόν εστιν). In the English Versions 'as it is meet' looks like a mere repetition of 'we are bound,' but this is not the case. 'We are bound' means 'conscience tells us that it is a debt to God'; 'as is meet' means 'it is only fair to you.' Lueken regards it as a natural addition in a Pauline letter; 'we are bound, and it is a worthy thing to do.' It is fanciful to suppose that this alludes to a letter from the Thessalonians in which they said that they did not deserve the praise given to them in 1 Thess. See on iii. 3, and cf. Phil. i. 7 καθώς ἐστιν δίκαιον. Except in 1 Timothy, ἄξιος is rare in Paul; and elsewhere in N.T. ἄξιον occurs only 1 Cor. xvi. 4.

we feel bound, I say] The insertion of these words is necessary in order to make clear that 'because' belongs to 'feel bound to thank' rather than to 'fair to you.'

faith . . . love] In 1 Thess. i. 3 all three of the great

Christian virtues are commended, faith, love, and hope. Here patient endurance (which is really *hopeful* endurance) under persecution takes the place of hope.

continues to increase more and yet more] A strong compound verb (ὑπεραυξάνει) is used. It occurs nowhere else in N.T., but is of a kind of which St. Paul is fond, viz., words compounded with ὑπέρ, *e.g.* ὑπεραίρεσθαι, ὑπεράνω, ὑπερβάλλω, ὑπερβαλλόντως, ὑπερεκπερισσοῦ, ὑπερεκτείνειν, ὑπερεντυγχάνειν, ὑπερέχειν, ὑπερλίαν, ὑπερνικᾷν, ὑπερπερισσεύειν, ὑπερπλεονάζειν. It indicates ceaseless organic growth, as of a healthy plant. These compounds perhaps are, as Lünemann suggests, "an involuntary expression of his overflowing feelings." Chrysostom and Oecumenius call attention to the compound here.

love continues to be more and more widely diffused] This increase in love St. Paul had prayed for in the earlier letter (iii. 12), and he would be therefore all the more thankful for its abundant manifestation. Here we have a slight indication that 2 Thess. was written after 1 Thess., and not before it, as Ewald and one or two other critics have thought. Love was specially needed in a young Church which had both Jews and Greeks among its members. 'Love' (R.V.) here and elsewhere is the better rendering of ἀγάπη. A.V. wavers between 'charity' and 'love' (ii. 10, iii. 5; 1 Thess. v. 8, etc.). 'Love of the brethren' (φιλαδελφία) abounded (iv. 10); but it is a less extensive term than 'love.'

The verb for 'increase' in this case (πλεονάζει) is in N.T. almost confined to the Pauline Epistles, but it is not rare elsewhere. It indicates spreading, as of fire or water, whether for good or for evil, rather than internal growth, as of an organism. Christian love does not pick and choose, refusing this or that person; it overflows all, even the disorderly idlers.

You yourselves doubtless rejoice at this] This is implied in the emphatic position of the pronouns which follow (ὥστε αὐτοὺς ἡμᾶς); 'so that we on our part, we as well as you, are affected.' The three missionaries were proud of the behaviour of their converts, which was no doubt a satisfaction to the converts themselves. All rejoiced together. *In laudandis Dei beneficiis semper respicienda est Ecclesiae universitas* (Calvin). Cf. the glowing words in 1 Thess. ii. 19.

4. **to glory about you**] As a rule, it was not expedient for the Apostle to glory (2 Cor. xii. 1) about God's favours, enabling him to win so many successes and endure so many sufferings. But there were times when the needs of his converts, or the criticisms of his enemies, drove him to do so (2 Cor. viii. 1–7; xi. 17, 21). In the present case it would be an encouragement to the Thessalonians to know that the founders of their Church took so much pride in it, and it would be a stimulus to other congregations to know what progress the Thessalonians were making. The compound ἐνκαυχᾶσθαι is rare in Bibl. Greek.

in the Christian congregations] These would be chiefly 'the saints which are in the whole of Achaia' (2 Cor. i. 1), especially Corinth and the neighbouring towns. Of course he does not mean *all* Christian congregations; cf. 1 Cor. xi. 16. There is little doubt that Polycarp had this passage in his mind when he wrote to the Philippians (xi. 3) about St. Paul "glorying in all the Churches." In xi. 4 he has an echo of 2 Thess. iii. 15. For 'the Churches of God' (αἱ ἐκκλησίαι τοῦ Θεοῦ) cf. 1 Thess. ii. 14; 1 Cor. xi. 16. 'The Church of God' (ἡ ἐκκλησία τ. Θ.) is very frequent (1 Cor. i. 2, x. 32, xv. 9; 2 Cor. i. 1; Gal. i. 13; cf. 1 Tim. iii. 5, 15), and both expressions are peculiar to Paul. The genitive is possessive, and it is probable that nowhere is it merely an otiose amplification. The point here may be that Christian and not Jewish or Greek assemblies are meant. The reading in Acts xx. 28 is rather uncertain, for authorities there are somewhat evenly divided; 'the Church of *the Lord*' (a unique expression) may there be right. See Briggs, *The Messiah of the Apostles*, pp. 81, 82.

the strength of your endurance] Patient and hopeful endurance (ὑπομονή) is a virtue on which great stress is laid in the N.T. and in early Christian writings in times of persecution. The word is frequent in the Pauline Epistles and in the Apocalypse, and what follows here has no parallel in 1 Thess. i. In 1 Tim. vi. 11; 2 Tim. iii. 10; Tit. ii. 2 it is combined, as here, with love and faith; and in Rom. xv. 5 we have the remarkable expression 'the God of patient endurance' (ὁ Θεὸς τῆς ὑπομονῆς). Calvin remarks that endurance is the fruit and evidence of faith, and here both are coupled under one article. Endurance is also closely connected with hope. In the O.T. it commonly means patient *expectation*; so even in Ecclus. ii. 14, xvi. 13, xvii. 24, xli. 2. But in 4 Maccabees, which was written not long before this Epistle, the N.T. signification occurs; τῇ ἀνδρείᾳ καὶ τῇ ὑπομονῇ i. 11; ἀρετὴ δὲ δι' ὑπομονῆς δοκιμάζουσα xvii. 12, also xvii. 23. Perhaps throughout the N.T. it implies an expectation that the suffering will prove a blessing, a hope that sorrow will be turned into joy. The word is found in all groups of the Pauline Epistles, implying manly endurance without cowardly shrinking. See Trench, *Syn.* § liii.; Ellicott on 1 Thess. i. 3; Cremer, *Lexicon*, p. 420; Abbott, *Son of Man*, p. 696.

in all the persecutions] These had been numerous and had not ceased. Both Jews and heathen were actively hostile (1 Thess. i. 6, ii. 14). The Jews followed the missionaries after they had fled, and they incited the 'more noble' Jews of Beroea to turn against them. See Lightfoot, *Biblical Essays*, pp. 262 f. The fact that 'faith' in *v.* 3 must mean belief in God and in Christ forbids us from giving 'faith' in *v.* 4 the sense of 'faithfulness' or 'constancy,' although that meaning would agree well with the idea of good conduct under persecution. In Bibl. Grk. διωγμός commonly means 'persecution,' not 'pursuit'; 2 Macc. xii. 23 ἐποιεῖτο δὲ τὸν διωγμὸν εὐτονώτερον, of Judas Maccabeus pursuing his enemies, is an exception.

the afflictions] A more general term than 'persecutions.' We have the two words combined Mk. iv. 17 = Mt. xiii. 21, γενομένης θλίψεως ἢ διωγμοῦ. Cf. διωκόμενοι ἀνεχόμεθα 1 Cor. iv. 12, and the Beatitude in Mt. v. 10. Θλίψις (or θλῖψις) occurs in all the Pauline groups, except the Pastorals

In class. Grk. it is perhaps not earlier than Aristotle, who uses it only in the original sense of 'pressure' or 'crushing.' A.V. varies between 'tribulation' and 'trouble' and 'affliction'; R.V. between 'tribulation' and 'affliction' and (Jn. xvi. 21) 'anguish'; Vulg. between *tribulatio* and *pressura* and (Col. i. 24) *passio*.

are still enduring] Persecution had probably continued since 1 Thessalonians was written, and the converts certainly had afflictions to endure. '*All* your persecutions and afflictions' implies repetition; and the present tenses (ἀνέχεσθε, and πάσχετε *v.* 5) imply that they continue; cf. 1 Thess. i. 6, ii. 14. On the apparent attraction to θλίψεσιν in αἷς ἀνέχεσθε see A. T. Robertson, *Grammar of the Greek N.T.*, p. 716. The words are "not otiose, but add weight and point to ὑπομονῆς" (Swete).

i. 5–10. Doctrine of the Righteousness of God's Judgment

There is no real break between *v.* 4 and *v.* 5, although the A.V. has a full stop. The semi-colon of the R.V. is almost too much, for 'a manifest token' is in apposition with the sense of *v.* 4, viz. the Thessalonians' patient endurance under persecution. A dash or line would express this better than a stop, but the insertion of 'which is' (A.V., R.V.) is legitimate.

5 *Which is* a manifest token of the righteous judgment of God, that ye may be counted worthy of the kingdom of God, for which ye also suffer; 6 Seeing it is a righteous thing with God to recompense tribulation to them that trouble you: 7 And to you who are troubled, rest with us, when the Lord Jesus shall be revealed from heaven, with his mighty Angels, 8 In flaming fire, taking vengeance on them that know not God, and that obey not the Gospel of our Lord Jesus Christ, 9 Who shall be punished with everlasting destruction from the presence of the Lord, and from the glory of his power: 10 When he shall come to be glorified in his Saints, and to be admired in all them that believe (because our testimony among you was believed) in that day.

This long sentence of six verses must be broken up in

paraphrasing. With the doctrine of Divine retribution and reward as set forth in these verses cf. Rev. vi. 10, xi. 18, xiii. 10, xvi. 4–7, xviii. 6–8. It constitutes the first part of St. Paul's apocalypse and leads on naturally to the second part in ii. 1–12. The contents of both are in the main either a repetition of Christ's teaching on the subject, or a deduction from it; but there are one or two new elements. We hardly do justice to the current of St. Paul's thought if we isolate ii. 1–12, as if it were a needless intrusion.

[5] We have mentioned our admiration of your patient endurance and stedfast faith, because this conduct of yours is such a clear demonstration that the Judge of all the earth is righteous in His judgment, for it tends to show that all those who have suffered persecution for the truth's sake will be accounted by Him to be worthy of His Kingdom, entrance into which is won by your heroic endurance of prolonged suffering for the Kingdom's sake. [6] We assert this, because we assume, what you will readily grant, that it is a righteous thing in the court of God that in the life to come there should be full compensation for the inequalities and injustices of this life; that the persecutors who afflict you for your righteousness should themselves be made to suffer affliction for their iniquity; [7] and that you, who are plainly on God's side, for it is He who has enabled you to endure for the Gospel's sake, should have relief along with ourselves —you and we have been alike in suffering, and we shall be alike in being freed from it—through the great revealing of the Lord Jesus Christ, when He comes from heaven, accompanied by the angels who are the ministers of His power, [8] and surrounded by a blaze of flame. Then He will render full retribution to those who obstinately refuse to recognize God in nature, and to those who have heard the Gospel of our Lord Jesus Christ and yet refuse to comply with its demands, viz., faith in Him and obedience to His teaching. [9] These men are of such a character that they will have to pay a just penalty which will be no less than eternal ruin, banishment from the presence of the Lord and from the glory of His strength, [10] whenever He shall have appeared again to the world, to be glorified in those holy ones who in their characters are reflexions of His holiness, and to be marvelled at in all those who believed the Gospel, and therefore in you, because our testimony about the Gospel has been brought to you and believed by you. But for all this we must wait patiently until He comes again in that Day.

5. **a clear demonstration**] This term (ἔνδειγμα) is found here only in N.T. The Latin version of Theodore has

demonstrationem, Tertullian *ostentamen*, Vulgate *in exemplum*. In this late Greek it can hardly be distinguished from ἔνδειξις (Rom. iii. 25, 26; 2 Cor. viii. 24; Phil. i. 28), although the latter should mean the process of proving rather than the proof. God's judgment is proved to be righteous by the fact that those who are persecuted for the Gospel's sake are rewarded hereafter, while those who persecute them are punished. The article and the singular number (τῆς δικαίας κρίσεως) show that the final judgment is meant, not the partial judgments executed in this world. Phil. i. 28 is similar. There the Philippians' stedfastness in facing the attacks of their persecutors is a clear demonstration to their enemies that by their hostility they are bringing spiritual ruin on themselves, while the persecuted receive salvation. Rev. xiii. 10 probably means that those who persecute will suffer persecution. Cf. also Dives and Lazarus, and Rom. ii. 5.

The construction is unimportant; either as an accusative or an elliptic nominative, ἔνδειγμα is in apposition with the previous statement. The persecutions 'attest the equity of God' (Rutherford). These awkward constructions, as Zahn points out (*Intr.* I. p. 253) are signs of genuineness.

for it tends to show] With εἰς τό of the result cf. 2 Cor. viii. 6.

accounted worthy] See below on *v.* 11. The words here seem almost like an echo of the words of Christ recorded Lk. xx. 35, καταξιωθέντες τοῦ αἰῶνος ἐκείνου τυχεῖν καὶ τῆς ἀναστάσεως τῆς ἐκ νεκρῶν. 'To be worthy of the age to come' is a common expression with the Rabbis (Dalman, *The Words of Jesus*, p. 119); and Christ and His Apostle may be using current phraseology. Cf. θείας μερίδος κατηξιώθησαν, 4 Macc. xviii. 3. H. A. A. Kennedy, *St. Paul's Conceptions of the Last Things*, pp. 161, 287. Cf. St. Paul's hope 2 Tim. iv. 8.

His Kingdom] "This kingdom is the rule of God, whether in the human heart, or in society. It exists now, but it has its full realization in eternity. Some have to seek and gain it. Those who have gained it have to labour to retain it, and this retaining may be regarded as winning it. It is to be noted that Christ never gave any definition of the kingdom, and perhaps it is not wise for us to attempt to do so" (Plummer on Mt. iii. 1–12, p. 25: see also A. Robertson, *Regnum Dei*, Bampton Lectures 1901, pp. 75–77; and for St. Paul's equivalent, Sanday in the *Journal of Theol. Stud.*, July 1900, p. 481.

for the Kingdom's sake] This is an important condition. The mere endurance of suffering does not necessarily secure entrance into the Kingdom. *Confirmantur in spe aeternae vitae dum pro ea militant* (Calvin). It is a great help towards the patient and hopeful endurance of suffering to be able to perceive that suffering is a benefit to us. Cf. Lk. vi. 23.

6. **we assume what you will readily grant**] 'If so be' (R.V.) is more accurate than 'Seeing it is' (A.V.), but the latter is legitimate, because the Apostle means that the supposition is not likely to be disputed. The change from 'tribulation' to 'trouble' (A.V.) spoils the verbal effect of 'affliction to them that afflict,' τοῖς θλίβουσιν θλίψιν.* The Greeks had a proverb which is similar, but more comprehensive, 'the doer must suffer,' δράσαντι παθεῖν, whatever a man sows he will reap. Cf. Mt. xxvii. 52; Rom. ii. 5; 2 Cor. v. 10; Eph. vi. 8; Col. iii. 24, 25; Rev. xiii. 2.

In N.T. εἴπερ is peculiar to Paul, and it is very rare in LXX. See Sanday and Headlam, *Romans*, p. 96.

Suggestions that 6–10 is an interpolation (McGiffert, *Enc. Bibl.* 5044), or an adaptation of a Christian hymn or Jewish apocalypse (Moffatt, *Literature of the N.T.*, p. 80, Findlay, Way, etc.), are sufficiently answered by Frame. They need not detain us. We have here "the free composition of Paul, influenced by O.T. and later Jewish literature."

* Vulg. has *tribulationem . . . tribulant*, Beza *afflictionem . . . affligunt*. The exactitude of the *lex talionis* as having Divine sanction is often pointed out; Gen. ix. 6; Exod. xxi. 12, 14; Lev. xxiv. 17; Is. lxvi. 4, 14 f.; especially in Wisdom xi. 16, xii. 23, xvi. 1, xviii. 4, 5. See Charles, *Book of Jubilees*, p. 42.

in the court of God] 'In His presence' (παρὰ Θεῷ), *i.e.* before Him as Judge. Cf. Rom. ii. 11, 13, where we have παρά in both verses.

full compensation] We again have a strong compound verb (ἀνταποδοῦναι). It and other words in the passage show how full the Apostle's mind was of the language of the LXX. The verb is used of requiting bad conduct, as here and Rom. xii. 19, and also of requiting good, as 1 Thess. iii. 9 (see note) and Rom. xi. 35; in both cases, of requiting *in full*.

7. **relief**] 'Release,' slackening of pressure, especially the pressure of affliction; 2 Cor. ii. 12, vii. 5, viii. 13; Acts xxiv. 23. As 'affliction' (θλίψις) implies crushing or constraint, so 'relief' (ἄνεσις) implies loosening or liberty. Beza has *relaxatio*, which is better than *requies* (Vulg.). In Ecclus. xv. 20, xxvi. 10, and in Barnabas iv. 10, it means freeing from wholesome restraint, licence. Cf. the Beatitudes, Mt. v. 10–12, also Job iii. 17 and Acts iii. 19. In Rev. xiv. 11 'rest' (ἀνάπαυσις) has a similar meaning.

In Scripture there is no promise that in this world there will ever be an abolition of suffering; what is offered is the alleviation which comes through our submission and Divine consolation. The abolition comes at the great Day. See Swete on Rev. vii. 17 and xxi. 4.

"This is the only passage in which Paul welcomes God's vengeance on the enemies of the church as an element in the recompense of Christians . . . He consoles the Thessalonians by depicting the doom of their opponents" (Moffatt). Cf. 'When the wicked are cut off, thou shalt see it' Ps. xxxvii. 34. But the fact of God's requital of sinners is frequently noted by St. Paul; 1 Cor. iii. 17; 2 Cor. xi. 15; Gal. v. 10; 2 Tim. iv. 14; etc. In 4 Ezra vii. 80–99 the seven miseries of the wicked in the intermediate state, and the seven joys of the righteous are described. The second joy of "those who have kept the ways of the Most High" is that "they see the circuit in which the souls of the ungodly wander, and the punishment that awaits them." Nowhere is this horrible thought found in St. Paul. What we have here is parallel to the Syriac Apocalypse of Baruch lxxxii. 1, which may be of about the same date as our Epistle; "Therefore, my brethren, I have written to you, that ye may comfort yourselves regarding the multitude of your tribulations. For know ye that our Maker will assuredly avenge us on all our enemies, according to all that they have done to us, also that the consummation which the Most High will make is very nigh, and His mercy that is coming, and the consummation of His judgment is by no means far off." The Apostle speaks often about the future joys of the righteous, seldom about the future punishment of the wicked. Cf. *Apoc. of Baruch* xv. 7, 8, xlviii. 48–50, li. 14, and esp. lii. 5–7, which is worthy of St. Paul; "And as for the righteous, what will ye do now? Rejoice ye in the suffering which ye now suffer: but why do ye look for the decline of your enemies? Make ready your soul for that which is reserved for you, and prepare your souls for the reward which is laid up for you." Cf. 2 Tim. iv. 8.

along with ourselves] St. Paul, Silvanus, and Timothy knew what suffering for the Gospel was; Rom. viii. 35; 2 Cor. xii. 10; and the Apostle often points out that such suffering is rewarded by joy hereafter; Rom. viii. 17; 2 Cor. i. 7; Phil. i. 28–30; 2 Tim. ii. 12. Rom. viii. 18 παθήματα are requited with abundant δόξα, and 2 Cor. iv. 17 the same requital is promised for θλίψις. Part of the future joy is freedom from oppression. 'You, like ourselves, have suffered; you, like ourselves, will have rest.'

We often regard *death* as a time of release or rest; but here that is not the Apostle's idea. He and the Thessalonians hoped to live till the Lord appeared; and to die before that crisis would hardly be a relief. He did not wish to be released from the body by death, but to have in exchange a spiritual body, without dying. This would be true release, and it would be granted when the Lord came again.

"These two little words (μεθ' ἡμῶν) belong to the genuine Pauline touches for the sake of which no one, with any feeling for the way in which the mind of Paul works, can give up the authenticity of this brief epistle" (Von Dobschütz, quoted with approval by Frame).

A rhythmical swing may be traced in what follows, and A. S. Way calls it the "Hymn of the Second Coming," dividing it as such, and translating somewhat freely ;—

"The cleaving heavens shall disclose the Lord Jesus,
Attended by the angel-ministers of His power,
Encircled with glowing flame, etc."

But there is little evidence that St. Paul is quoting any such hymn or is consciously composing one. See on 1 Thess. iv. 17 ; also Ramsay, *The First Christian Century*, pp. 105–107 ; Swete, *The Life of the World to Come*, pp. 28, 33, 112.

the great revealing of the Lord Jesus] Here and elsewhere we may notice "the fearlessness with which the Apostle applies the phenomena represented in the O.T. as symbols of the Divine presence to the Appearing of our Lord" (Lightfoot) : cf. 1 Thess. iv. 16, 17 ; 1 Cor. xv. 52. In this he is following the example of Christ, who in His teaching about the Second Advent (Mk. xiii. 24–27 ; Mt. xxiv. 29–31 ; Lk. xxi. 25–27) uses freely the picturesque symbolical language which was current among the Jews at that time ; Is. xiii. 10, xxxiv. 4 ; Ezek. xxxii. 7, 8 ; Amos viii. 9 ; Joel ii. 30, 31, iii. 15. See notes on 1 Thess. iv. 16 ; also Charles, *Revelation*, pp. 3, 4.

'Revealing' or 'revelation' is mainly a Scriptural term, and its use in the N.T. to denote the Second Advent no doubt comes from our Lord's words as recorded Lk. xvii. 30, 'After the same manner shall it be in the day that the Son of man is revealed' (*ἀποκαλύπτεται*), "where it is to be noticed that the revelation is assigned to a Day, . . . that is, the Day is a Divine manifestation, a Day of the Lord . . . There is nothing in either this passage (1 Pet. i. 7) or others on the same subject, apart from the figurative language of Thess., to show that the revelation here spoken of is to be limited to a sudden preternatural theophany. It may be a long and varying process, though ending in a climax. Essentially it is simply the removal of the veils which hide the unseen Lord, by whatever means they may be withdrawn" (Hort on 1 Pet. i. 7, p. 44). See also Briggs,

The Messiah of the Apostles, pp. 90f. The word occurs thirteen times in the Pauline Epistles, and five times elsewhere; but only here and 1 Cor. i. 7 is it definitely used of the Second Advent, although Rom. ii. 5 and viii. 19 refer to the same event. See Westcott, *Intr. to the Study of the Gospels*, 7th ed. 1888, p. 9 note, and *Ephesians*, pp. 178 f. 'Revelation' (ἀποκάλυψις) is not found in the Pastoral Epistles, where its place is taken by 'appearing' or 'manifestation' (ἐπιφάνεια); see on ii. 8. 'Second Advent' is not found in Scripture, but it occurs Justin Martyr *Try.* 40; cf. 110, 121, and *Apol.* i. 52. See Milligan, *Thessalonians*, pp. 145 f. 'Revealing' is more definite than 'Coming'; it implies previous concealment, a mystery. In *v.* 4 we had ἐν thrice with different shades of meaning; here we have three different prepositions, ἀπ' οὐρανοῦ (Rom. i. 18), μετ' ἀγγέλων (Mk. viii. 38), and ἐν πυρὶ φλογός (Exod. iii. 2).

accompanied by the angels who are ministers of His power] 'With his mighty angels' (A.V.) is certainly wrong, although it is advocated by Jowett. 'Angels of power' might mean 'mighty angels,' on the analogy of the Hebraic or Oriental use of the genitive in place of an adjective (Winer, p. 297), like 'hearer of forgetfulness,' 'judges of evil thoughts' (Jas. i. 25, ii. 4). But 'angels of *His* power' (ἀγγέλων δυνάμεως αὐτοῦ) could not be thus used; the 'His' belongs to 'power' and not to 'angels.' 'His power' means the power of Jesus Christ, and the angels manifest it: *angelos potentiae vocat in quibus suam potentiam exseret* (Calvin); they are to execute His commands. In the Book of Enoch lxi. 10 we have 'angels of power' among the host of the heavens, and in the Testaments of the XII Patriarchs, *Judah* iii. 10, we have 'an angel of might.' In Christ's revelation of the Last Things the angels gather the elect, Mk. xiii. 27; Mt. xxiv. 31: here they execute judgment on the ungodly. But Christ had intimated both of these duties; Mt. xiii. 30, 41, xvi. 27.

8. **surrounded by a blaze of flame**] Lit. 'in a fire of flame' (ἐν πυρὶ φλόγος), as in Exod. iii. 2, which the Apostle has in his mind; cf. Ecclus. viii. 10, xlv. 24. In Acts vii. 30,

we have 'in a flame of fire' (ἐν φλογὶ πυρός); and φλὸξ πυρός prevails Rev. i. 14, ii. 18, xix. 12; also Ps. xxviii. (xxix.) 7 φωνὴ Κυρίου διακόπτοντος φλόγα πυρός. But in some of these passages the readings vary. The language of the LXX has influenced 2 Thessalonians less than 1 Thessalonians. There are apparent echoes in these verses, but the clearest instances are in the description of the Lawless One ii. 3–12; see also iii. 1. For theophanies in a blaze of fire cf. Exod xix. 18, xxiv. 17; 2 Chron. vii. 1; Ezek. i. 13, 27; Dan. vii. 9, 10; cf. Exod. xxxiv. 29; Num. xiv. 14.

The division between the verses at this point, making 'in flaming fire' part of *v.* 8, shows that those who made it regarded the 'flaming fire' as the instrument of vengeance on those who know not God. It is very doubtful whether this is meant even in a secondary degree. The primary meaning certainly is that the 'blaze of flame' is part of the overwhelming glory of the Lord's presence, such as had blinded the Apostle himself when he was on the way to Damascus. As has been pointed out just above, in the O.T. we often have fire as a symbol of the Divine Presence; there of Jehovah, as here of Christ. Clemen needlessly suggests that St. Paul "here assumes that this world will perish by burning" (*Primitive Christianity and its non-Jewish Sources*, p. 161). See Deissmann, *St. Paul*, p. 191.

will render] Grammatically this cannot be taken with flame, for the participle (διδόντος) is masculine, and flame (φλόξ) is feminine. Even if ἐν φλογὶ πυρός were the right reading, διδόντος must certainly be taken with **τοῦ Κυρίου Ἰησοῦ**.

full retribution] This rather than 'vengeance' (A.V., R.V.), which suggests vindictiveness and revenge, is the meaning of ἐκδίκησις. But 'vengeance' is normal as a rendering; Lk. xviii. 7, 8, xxi. 22; Rom. xii. 19; 2 Cor. vii. 11; 1 Pet. ii. 14. Here again we have, attributed to Christ, what in Deut. xxxii. 35 (quoted Heb. x. 20) is said to be reserved for Jehovah. "Inevitable retribution is conspicuous in the epistles of Paul;" cf. Rom. ii. 5, 7–10;

also Acts xvii. 31, xxiv. 15, "the only references to the Second Coming of Christ in Paul's recorded speeches" (Beet, *Last Things*, pp. 11, 48; see also Plummer on 2 Cor. v. 10). In the Book of Enoch the 'Elect One' or the 'Son of Man' sits on the throne of His glory to judge; lv. 4, lxii. 3, 5. He has been placed there by the Lord of Spirits, and all judgment has been committed to Him; li. 3, lxii. 2, lxix. 27, 29. See Charles on xlv. 3.

It is of His own nature that God is a God of love; it is because of the existence of sin that He is also a God of 'vengeance'; Ps. xliii. 1; Nah. i. 2; Is. lix. 18. See St. Bernard, *In Nativ. Dom. Serm.* v. 3.

those who . . . those who] It is not quite certain whether we have here two distinct classes of persons, or the same class described in two different ways. In strict grammar the repetition of the article (*τοῖς μὴ εἰδόσι Θεὸν καὶ τοῖς μὴ ὑπακούουσιν*) requires us to distinguish two classes; and these would be the heathen who had never heard the Gospel and had ignored the truths of Natural Religion (Acts xiv. 17), and the Jews and heathen who had had the Gospel preached to them and had rejected it. But the whole passage is very Hebraic in tone, and we may have here an instance of the parallelism which is so characteristic of Hebrew poetry and prophecy, where the same fact or person or class is often described in two different ways; *e.g.* Pss. lxiv., lxv., lxvi.: Jer. x. 25, xiv. 7–9, xvi. 5, xvii. 1; etc. See esp. Ps. cxlix. 7 *τοῦ ποιῆσαι ἐκδίκησιν εν τοῖς ἔθνεσιν, ἐλεγμοὺς ἐν τοῖς λαοῖς.* On the whole, it is safest to distinguish two classes, and regard the similar expressions for the heathen in 1 Thess. iv. 5 and Gal. iv. 8 as parallel to the first expression here. Rom. i. 18–32 shows the consequences of refusing to recognize God in His works. The A.V., by not repeating 'to them,' makes only one class; the R.V. repeats 'to them,' and thus seems to make two classes, but the second may be another description of the same class of sinners. The participles, as usual in N.T., have *μή* and not *οὐ*: cf. iii. 11. Winer, p. 596.

9. **of such a character**] The qualitative relative (*οἵτινες*) may here have its full force, as often in the Pauline Epistles; Rom. i. 25, 32, ii. 15; 1 Cor. iii. 17, v. 1; 2 Cor. viii. 10; Eph. iv. 19, etc. It is not merely 'who,' but 'who are of such a quality as.' In late Greek this refinement is lost; but in N.T. there are many passages in which it still survives, as here. See Lightfoot on Gal. iv. 27 and Phil. i. 28.

pay a just penalty] Or 'suffer a just punishment' (*δίκην τίσουσιν*). The phrase is unique in N.T., but is frequent in classical Greek. See abundant examples in Wetstein. In N.T. the substantive is rare (Acts xxviii. 4 of Justice personified, and Jude 7) and the verb does not occur. Cf. Prov. xxvii. 12 *ἄφρονες δὲ ζημίαν τίσουσιν.*

Δίκη meant originally 'right as determined by custom,' then 'right as determined by law'; hence 'legal process for determining right,' 'lawsuit' or 'trial'; finally the result of such trial, 'satisfaction' or 'penalty.' Other words for 'chastisement' or 'punishment' are rare in N.T.; *κόλασις* only Mt. xxv. 46 and 1 Jn. iv. 18; *τιμωρία* only Heb. x. 29; *ζημία* only Acts xxvii. 10, 21; Phil. iii. 7, 8.

eternal ruin] The expression (*ὄλεθρον αἰώνιον*) is found nowhere else in N.T., and nowhere else does St. Paul speak of 'ruin' or 'perdition' as being 'eternal.' The expression occurs 4 Macc. x. 15 of the future fate of the tyrant Antiochus. The two words (*ὄλεθρον καὶ ἀπώλειαν*) occur together 1 Tim. vi. 9. The Apostle does not say much about 'those who are perishing' (*οἱ ἀπολλύμενοι*): his chief interest is in 'those who are being saved' (*οἱ σωζόμενοι*). Hastings' *D.B.*, I. p. 755b. Few changes in the R.V. are more important than the substitution of 'eternal' for 'everlasting' as the translation of *αἰώνιος*, which *need* not mean more than 'age-long,' 'lasting for an age,' the length of the age depending upon the context. In inscriptions and papyri it often means 'lifelong,' especially in reference to the life of a Caesar. In N.T., where it is commonly used in reference to 'the age to come' in contrast to 'this age,' the rendering 'eternal' is specially appropriate. But that 'eternal' necessarily means 'everlasting' is more than we know or have the right to assert. 'Eternity,' though positive in form, is negative in meaning; it is something which cannot be measured by clocks and calendars. It would be rash to say that in N.T. 'eternal' never means 'endless,' 'lasting for an infinite number of infinite ages,' but it would be still more rash to say that it always means this, as the rendering 'everlasting' implies. 'Eternal ruin' is preferable to 'eternal destruction' (R.V.), which might be supposed to mean the *annihilation* of the obstinate unbelievers and the wilfully disobedient, an idea which cannot be attributed to St. Paul. Disastrous loss seems to be implied rather than the extinction of existence. Swete points out that Theodore, following Diodore of Tarsus, held the future punishment of the wicked to be remissible on their repentance. But he may have regarded it as objectively eternal, as it belongs to a life not measured by periods of time. See Kennedy, *St. Paul's Conceptions of the Last Things*, pp. 314 f.; Beet, *Last Things*, pp. 132 f.

banishment from the presence of the Lord] 'Banishment' is not expressed in the Greek, and there is some doubt as to the word which is understood. Some amplification is necessary in thought, if not in language, for 'eternal ruin from the presence of the Lord' is ambiguous. Is. ii. 10, 19, 21 seems to be in the Apostle's mind, and in those verses 'from' certainly means 'separation from.' This is a point strongly in favour of taking 'from' (ἀπό) here in the *local* sense of 'banishment from'; and this makes excellent sense. It was the joy of the genuine believer to look forward to the Lord's Return as the beginning of the exquisite experience of 'being for ever with the Lord' (1 Thess. iv. 17*). It would be the special misery of those who had refused to believe, that they would be eternally banished from the face of the Lord. Cf. 'The face of the Lord is against them that do evil,' 'Who may stand in Thy sight when once Thou art angry?' (Ps. xxxiv. 16, lxxvi. 7), and 'Depart from

* Cf. Ps. xi. 7, xvii. 5; Mt. v. 8, xviii. 10; Heb. xii. 14; Rev. xxii. 4.

Me, all ye workers of iniquity' (Lk. xiii. 27; Mt. xxv. 41); also 'the outer darkness' (Mt. xxii. 13, xxv. 30). In 'the Parables' in the Book of Enoch (xxxvii.–lxxi.) the Righteous One, or Elect One, or Son of Man, is seated on the throne of His glory to judge men and angels; xl. 1, lxii. 2–5, lxix. 27–29. This Jewish idea would be familiar to St. Paul, who would see in it "a true and abiding idea, which, if purified and vivified, must take its place in Christian eschatology" (Rostron, *The Christology of St. Paul*, p. 54).

Two other explanations of 'from' (ἀπό) are possible. It may mean 'proceeding from.' This would imply that the full retribution rendered to the unbelieving and the disobedient proceeds from, and is produced by, the face of the Lord and the glory of His strength. The mere revealing of the Divine Presence and Power involves eternal ruin to those who have hitherto persistently ignored the Presence and resisted the Power. Both grammatically and intrinsically this *causal* interpretation is less probable than the local sense. But it is quite tenable, and some commentators prefer it.

The third explanation of 'from' is that it has a *temporal* signification,—'from the *time* of the Lord's Presence.' This hardly fits the context; and, if this had been meant, some other word than 'face' would have been used to express the Divine Presence. This explanation may safely be set on one side.

Not more than a comma must be placed at the end *v.* 9. What follows is closely connected with *v.* 9, and grammatically it is part of the same sentence.

10. **whenever He shall have appeared again**] It is certain that He will appear again, and that what has just been stated will result from His appearing; but the exact moment is uncertain. Cf. Mk. xiv. 62; Acts. i. 11; Rev. i. 7; and see on 1 Thess. iv. 16.

to be glorified] This is the object of His appearing. The verb is a compound (ἐνδοξασθῆναι) which occurs again in *v.* 12, but nowhere else in N.T. In the LXX it is fairly common, and the Apostle may be thinking of Ps. lxxxviii.

(lxxxix.) 8, ὁ Θεὸς ἐνδοξαζόμενος ἐν βουλῇ ἁγίων, 'God is very greatly to be feared in the council of the saints,' or 'very terrible in the council of the holy ones.' In N.T. 'the saints' (οἱ ἅγιοι) commonly means those who as Christians have been consecrated to God and are bound to live holy lives; and some make these, and these only, to be the meaning here. The 'angels of His power' are ministers of wrath to punish the disobedient, and 'His saints' are the holy men and women who are the mirrors of His glory. E. A. Abbott, *The Son of Man*, pp. 223, 293. But in LXX and subsequent Jewish writings angels are often called 'the holy ones.' It is possible, therefore, that here, as in 1 Thess. iii. 13, they are to be included along with redeemed men and women. This glorious company of angels and good Christians is the sphere *in* which the glorifying of the Lord takes place. Cf. 'I am glorified in them,' Jn. xvii. 1; also xiii. 31, xiv. 13; Gal. i. 24; 1 Pet. iv. 11. Their holiness has its source in His and reflects His, and thus it is a glory to Him.

and to be marvelled at] An Hebraic parallel to the previous statement. Cf. Ps. lxvii. 36 (lxviii. 35) θαυμαστὸς ὁ Θεὸς ἐν τοῖς ὁσίοις αὐτοῦ, but there it is holy *places*, and not holy persons, that are mentioned. 'Admired' (A.V.) is one of many words which has had its meaning modified since 1611. Originally it expressed astonishment and amazement, which *might* be the reverse of admiration; * and 'admired' is now too weak, even where the amazement does imply joyous approbation. Wright, *Bible Word Book*, p. 12; Trench, *Select Glossary*, p. 2; Davies, *Bible English*, p. 143. Here earlier English Versions have 'made wondirful' (Wiclif), or 'made mavelous' (Tyndale, Genevan, Rhemish); Vulg., *admirabilis fieri*. Cf. Wisd. viii 11; Ecclus. xxxviii. 3.

those who believed] This expression (οἱ πιστεύσαντες) occurs Heb. iv. 3 and Acts iv. 32; cf. 1 Cor. xv. 2. It regards faith in its critical action at the time when the Gospel was accepted. The more usual expressions are

* Thus Jeremy Taylor says that "in man there is nothing admirable but his ignorance."

πεπιστευκότες (Acts xviii. 27, xix. 18, xxi. 20, 25; Tit. iii. 8), which includes the present result of the previous acceptance, and *οἱ πιστεύοντες* (1 Thess. i. 7, ii. 10, 13; Rom. iv. 24; 1 Cor. i. 25, xiv. 22; Eph. i. 19; etc.), which regards faith in its continuous exercise. Westcott on Heb. iv. 3. All three expressions point to a definite class. The A.V. here has 'believe,' following a false reading.

It is not likely that 'those who believed' means ordinary Christians, as distinct from 'His holy ones,' meaning exceptionally holy ones, viz. angels and saints. This is against the usage of St. Paul, who regards all Christians as 'called to be saints.' It is, however, possible that the twofold expression here is meant to be the antithesis of the twofold expression in *v.* 8, 'His holy ones' being the opposite of 'those who refuse to recognize God' and 'those who believed' the opposite of 'those who refuse to obey.' It is *τοῖς πιστεύσασιν* that suggests *ἐπιστεύθη* (or *ἐπιστῴθη*) in what follows, just as *πίστις* suggests *πιστός* in iii. 2, 3.

because our testimony . . . believed by you] This is an awkward parenthesis, interjected to show that the Thessalonians will have a share in the marvellous glory; they of course are included in 'all those who believed.' The Greek construction is not easy; Winer, p. 326; A.T. Robertson, *Gr. of the Grk. N.T.*, p. 485. The sense is much the same whether we take 'unto you' (*ἐφ' ἡμᾶς*) with the nominative (*τὸ μαρτύριον ἡμῶν*) or with the verb (*ἐπιστεύθη*). Bengel's 'as *far* as you, who are in the West' has little point, and gives an unnatural meaning to *ἐπί*. Westcott and Hort conjecture *ἐπιστώθη* (found in cursive 31) as possibly the right reading,—'was confirmed upon you,' or 'towards you.'

in that Day] The Vulgate here goes wrong with its unintelligent punctuation; so also Pelagius and his followers. These words do not belong to the parenthesis respecting the Thessalonians, in which they would be meaningless, but to the clauses which precede the parenthesis; 'to be glorified . . . and to be marvelled at . . . in that Day.' The words come at the end of the sentence with much emphasis. 'That Day' (*ἡ ἡμέρα ἐκείνη*) is Pauline of the

Day of Judgment (2 Tim. i. 12, 18, iv. 8), and apparently comes from the Lord Himself; Mk. xiii. 32, xiv. 25; Mt. xxiv. 36; Lk. x. 12, xxi. 34. Cf. Joel iii. 18; Obad. 8; Zeph. i. 10, 12; Zech. ii. 11, etc. See Westcott on Heb. x. 25.

Here the long sentence which began at *v.* 3 comes to an end; and, like the two remaining divisions of the letter, it ends with intercession for those to whom it is addressed. The whole passage illustrates the joy which the first Christians felt under persecution, owing to their glowing hopes with regard to future reward. *Les faits matériels des origines chrétiennes sont presque tous obscurs; ce qui est clair, c'est l'enthousiasme ardent, la hardiesse surhumaine, le sublime mépris de la réalité, qui font de ce mouvement le plus puissant effort vers l'idéal dont le souvenir ait été conservé* (Renan, *L'Antechrist*, p. iii.). *Ce qui est clair, ce qui explique le succès inoui de la propagande chrétienne, c'est l'esprit de dévouement, de haute moralité qui régnait dans ces petites Églises* (Renan, *Saint Paul*, p. 256).

11, 12. PRAYER FOR THE THESSALONIANS

The frequency with which the Apostle's teaching passes into prayer illuminates his charge to 'pray without ceasing' (1 Thess. v. 17). He recognizes that his words will have little effect unless 'God gives the increase' (1 Cor. iii. 6); and the Spirit of prayer is behind all that he says and does.

11 Wherefore also we pray always for you, that our God would count you worthy of this calling, and fulfil all the good pleasure of *his* goodness, and the work of faith with power: 12 That the Name of our Lord Jesus Christ may be glorified in you, and ye in him, according to the grace of our God, and the Lord Jesus Christ.

The way in which the opening Thanksgiving quickly suggests prayer for the converts should be compared with the similar transitions in Col. i. 9 and Phil. i. 9; see also 1 Thess. iii. 9–13; Eph. i. 16, 17.

11 And in order to promote your being pronounced by God to be worthy of His Kingdom and all its glories, we on all occasions add to our thanksgivings our earnest prayers on your behalf, that He who is

both our God and yours may account *you* worthy of the calling into His Kingdom, which He gave to you at your conversion, and which we trust will be repeated, in accordance with your hopes, when the Lord Jesus returns. To this end may He fulfil in you every degree of delight in well-doing and every degree of activity as proof of your faith. May He do this mightily ; [12] with the blessed result that the excellence which is implied in the Name of our Lord Jesus may be glorified by being manifested in you, and ye may be glorified in Him, in accordance with the gracious favour shown to us by our God and by the Lord Jesus Christ.

11. **And in order to**] 'Wherefore' (A.V.) is inadequate for *Εἰς ὅ*: 'To which end' (R.V.) is much better. Cf. *εἰς τό* with the infinitive i. 5, ii. 2, 6, 10, 11, iii. 9; etc. As the thanksgiving on the Thessalonians' behalf was offered 'on all occasions' (*v.* 3), so 'on all occasions' intercession for them is added. On the construction see A. T. Robertson, *Gr. of the Grk. N.T.*, p. 714. Note the alliteration with *π*, of which St. Paul is fond, *προσευχόμεθα πάντοτε περί*; cf. 2 Cor. ix. 5, 8, x. 6; Col. i. 3; etc.

both our God and yours] After 'on your behalf' we might have expected '*your* God'; but by means of this change the Apostle intimates once more how closely he is united with his converts. Cf. 1 Thess. i. 9, 10, where after '*ye* turned' we have 'delivered *us*'; iv. 6, where after 'each one of *you*' we have 'called *us*'; and v. 5, where after 'ye are all' we have '*we* are.' 'Our God' occurs 1 Thess. ii. 2, iii. 9. St. Paul more often says 'my God'; Rom. i. 8; 1 Cor. i. 4; 2 Cor. xii. 21; Phil. i. 3, iv. 19; Philem. 4.

add to our thanksgivings] This is implied in 'we *also* pray' (*καὶ προσευχόμεθα*). Others understand the *καί* as meaning 'we too as well as you pray'; but this does not imply that the Thessalonians had written to this effect: see on 1 Thess. ii. 13.

on your behalf] Lit. 'about you' (*περὶ ὑμῶν*), *i.e.* 'thinking about you when we pray.' See on 1 Thess. v. 10, 35; there we have a similar use of *περί* where *ὑπέρ* might seem to be more appropriate. See Lightfoot on Gal. i. 4; Winer, pp. 466 f.

may account you worthy] The verb (*ἀξιόω*) never means

'*make* worthy,' but always '*account* worthy,' 'reckon or treat as worthy'; and in N.T. it is commonly associated, as here, with the thought of a benefit or requital; Lk. vii. 7; 1 Tim. v. 17; Heb. iii. 3. In Heb. x. 29 the requital is punishment. Cf. δικαιόω, which does not mean 'make righteous,' but 'account righteous.' Material qualities can be given; λευκόω 'I make white,' λειόω 'I make smooth,' πληρόω 'I make full'; but moral qualities cannot be bestowed. We can account a man to be honest and true, and we can treat him as such; but we cannot give him these virtues. This distinction is of importance in determining the meaning of 'calling.' *Ante vocationem nulla dignitas in nobis* (Bengel). 'You' is emphatic by position, ἵνα ὑμᾶς ἀξιώσῃ. On the genitive with ἀξιόω see A. T. Robertson, *Gr. of Grk. N.T.*, p. 511.

the calling] This term and its cognate verb (κλῆσις, καλέω) are commonly used of the beginning of the Christian life, of being admitted into Christ's fold and called to be saints (Eph. iv. 1; 2 Tim. i. 9). That meaning may be the exclusive meaning here. But something future seems to be included, if not to prevail; 'that ye may be found worthy of that to which ye have been called' (Pelagius). The calling is the invitation to enter the Kingdom of God. That Kingdom is partly present and partly future. The domain in which God rules is partially realized in this world; and it will have its full development hereafter. St. Paul may be merely praying that God may count the Thessalonians as being worthy of having received His invitation to *enter the fold*. But the context appears to show that he includes, or even primarily means, the invitation to *enter the kingdom which will be inaugurated when the Lord Jesus is revealed in glory*. The A.V., with '*this* calling,' seems to decide for the latter. But 'this' is an exaggerated rendering of the Greek article (τῆς κλήσεως), where 'the calling' means 'the calling that is yours,' 'your calling' (R.V.).*

* Exaggerated renderings of the article are rather common in the A.V.; '*that* light,' Jn. i. 8; '*that* prophet,' i. 21, 25, vi. 14; '*that* bread,' vi. 48; '*that* Christ,' 69; '*this* way,' Acts ix. 2; '*that* way,' xix. 9, 23, xxiv. 22; etc.

The Greek article is often equivalent to a possessive pronoun. See on iii. 14.

We must be content to leave it doubtful whether the Apostle means the invitation to become Christians, or the invitation to enter into Christ's glory, or both.

may He fulfil in you] We might say 'may He fill you to the full with,' or 'may He bring to perfection'; but 'fulfil' is the normal rendering of πληρόω, which is very frequent in Gospels, Acts, and Pauline Epistles, and we need not displace it.

every degree of delight in well doing] Here the A.V. differs considerably from the R.V. It has 'all the good pleasure of *his* goodness,' viz. God's goodness, the italics showing that there is no 'his' in the Greek, which is simply πᾶσαν εὐδοκίαν ἀγαθωσύνης. The A.V. rendering is intelligible, but it can hardly be right. It is true that εὐδοκία is commonly used of God's 'good pleasure' or 'good-will' towards mankind (Lk. ii. 14; Eph. i. 5, 9; Phil. ii. 13), and at first sight it seems natural to take it in that sense here; cf. Ps. cv. (cvi.) 4, μνήσθητι ἡμῶν, Κύριε, ἐν τῇ εὐδοκίᾳ τοῦ λαοῦ σου. Hence the A.V. makes both the 'good pleasure' and the 'goodness' to be God's. But, for two reasons, this seems to be untenable. The 'work of faith' (ἔργον πίστεως), *i.e.* the good work which is the fruit of faith and the evidence that faith exists (Jas. ii. 17–26), must refer to the good actions and genuine faith of the Thessalonian converts; and consequently the 'good pleasure of goodness,' or 'desire of goodness' (R.V.) must be theirs also. We have here the progress of will (εὐδοκία) to deed (ἔργον). See Sanday and Headlam on Rom. x. 1, and Kennedy, *Sources of N.T. Greek*, p. 131. Secondly, ἀγαθωσύνη (Rom. xv. 14; Gal. v. 22; Eph. v. 9) seems always to be used of human goodness. One sinner will destroy ἀγαθωσύνην πολλήν Eccles. ix. 18. As distinct from δικαιοσύνη, it indicates the gentler side of the Christian character. It is the virtue of the generous and sympathetic man, whose chief desire is to be beneficent, and who is willing to make allowances; whereas the 'just' man thinks only of what can in strict fairness be claimed.

See Lightfoot on Rom. v. 7 and Gal. v. 22; also Trench, *Syn.* § 63. It is possible to interpret the genitive differently, 'good-will which springs from goodness,' or 'is inspired by goodness.' But the 'pleasure of good action,' or 'delight in well-doing' is better; cf. Rom. i. 32. Doing good is better than doing nothing; but to take delight in doing good is best of all. 'God loveth a cheerful giver,' 2 Cor. ix. 7.

every degree of activity] Although 'all' is feminine (πᾶσαν εὐδοκίαν) and is not repeated before 'activity' (ἔργον), yet it is to be understood; cf. ii. 4, 9; Rom. i. 29, xv. 13; and esp. Eph. iv. 31, where, as here and ii. 9, we have a change of gender, πᾶσα πικρία καὶ θυμός.

as proof of your faith] The only proof of the reality of faith is well-doing. 'Inspired by faith' is another possible rendering of the genitive. See on ii. 13. As in 1 Thess. i. 3, 'faith' here covers the whole life of the believer; and here, as in Gal. v. 6, St. Paul shows that he is at one with St. James (ii. 18–26) as to the necessary connexion between faith and works.

May He do this mightily] Like 'in that Day' (*v.* 10), 'with power' or 'mightily' (ἐν δυνάμει) comes at the end of a long sentence with special emphasis. But in English, in order to show clearly, that the emphatic expression belongs to 'fulfil,' and not to words that are nearer to it, it is almost necessary to make a separate sentence. Col. i. 29 we have the same adverbial expression at the end of a sentence. Cf. 1 Thess. i. 5; Rom. i. 4. *Nec temere dicit* cum potentia: *innuit enim fidei perfectionem rem esse arduam et summae difficultatis* (Calvin). Beza has *potenter.* Rutherford takes ἐν δυνάμει with ἔργον πίστεως, 'a faith achieving miracles,' which can hardly stand.

Findlay, followed by Milligan, quotes the Collect for Easter Week as a commentary on *v.* 11; "That as by Thy special grace preventing us Thou dost put into our minds good desires, so by Thy continual help we may bring the same to good effect."

12. **With the blessed result**] This explains the opening

words of *v.* 11. The 'that' in 'that He may account' (*v.* 11) is the exceedingly frequent ἵνα, which there, perhaps, may have its original sense of 'in order that.' Here, possibly to avoid a repetition of the same word, we have ὅπως, which is not nearly so frequent elsewhere, and is very rare in Paul. In 1 Cor. i. 29 ὅπως follows a threefold ἵνα, and in 2 Cor. viii. 14 a twofold ἵνα. See A. T. Robertson, *Gr.*, pp. 986 f., on the use of ὅπως in N.T., and cf. Jas. v. 16.

the Name of our Lord Jesus may be glorified] 'Christ' after 'Jesus' (A.V.) must be omitted as having no sufficient authority. Here again, as in *vv.* 7, 9, we have what is said in the O.T., of Jehovah transferred simply to Christ, as if the transfer was natural and required no explanation. In the O.T. 'the Name of The Lord' means the character and attributes of Jehovah so far as they have been made known. Cf. esp. Is. lxvi. 5 ἵνα τὸ ὄνομα Κυρίου δοξασθῇ, and Lev. xxiv. 11, 16, a misunderstanding of which made the Jews avoid uttering the word 'Yahve' or 'Jehovah.' See Hastings' *D.B.* art. 'Name,' pp. 478 f. Here 'the Name of our Lord Jesus' is used in a similar way; cf. Phil. ii. 9.

in you] Showing the close union which exists between the Head and the members, between the Vine and the branches. As in *v.* 10, His saints are the sphere *in* which the Lord is glorified. This may refer either to the admiration and joy which the progress of the Thessalonians excites in other Christians, causing them to praise Him, or possibly to the glorification of Christ in His holy ones at the Second Advent, or perhaps to both. Cf. Phil. i. 20; Jn. xxi. 19.

and ye may be glorified in Him] This reminds us of Jn. xv. 4–8, xvii. 10, 21–26. 'In Christ' occurs with great frequency in the Pauline Epistles. See on 1 Thess. iv. 16, and Sanday and Headlam on Rom. vi. 11. If ἐν αὐτῷ means 'in it,' viz. 'in the Name,' rather than 'in Him,' the meaning is much the same. St. Paul's 'in Christ' may have come from recollections of Christ's sayings; Jn. vi. 56, xiv. 20, xv. 4, 5, xvii. 21.

in accordance with the gracious favour] The Apostle is anxious to preserve the Thessalonians from supposing that their being glorified will be the result of their merits, as his mention of their delight in well-doing and the activity of their faith might lead them to think. It is all owing to the bounteous grace of God; ii. 16; Rom. iii. 24, v. 15, xi. 5, 6; Eph. i. 5, 6, ii. 5–9; etc. For *κατά* cf. ii. 3, iii. 6. See J. A. Robinson, *Ephesians*, p. 225.

shown to us by our God and by the Lord Jesus Christ] There is little doubt that this is the meaning of *τοῦ Θεοῦ ἡμῶν καὶ Κυρίου Ἰησοῦ Χριστοῦ*: the gracious favour is that of the Father and of the Son. But two other renderings are possible. We may limit the source of grace to the Father by making *ἡμῶν* and *Κυρίου Ἰ. Χρ.* parallel genitives after *τοῦ Θεοῦ*, 'God of us and of the Lord Jesus Christ; cf. Jn. xx. 17. Or again, we may limit the source of grace to the Son by making *τοῦ Θεοῦ ἡμῶν καὶ Κυρίου* refer to one Person, there being no article before *Κυρίου*, 'our God and Lord Jesus Christ.' But the omission of the article before *Κυρίου* does not show that this is intended, for *Κύριος* without the article is often treated as a proper name, and St. Paul commonly distinguishes the Father from the Christ by calling the former *Θεός* and the latter *Κύριος*, as i. 1; 1 Cor. i. 3; 2 Cor. i. 2; etc.; Tit. ii. 13 is similar, *τοῦ μεγάλου Θεοῦ καὶ σωτῆρος ἡμῶν Χριστοῦ Ἰησοῦ*, and there A.V. and R.V. margin give two Persons, while R.V. makes the whole refer to Jesus Christ. In 2 Pet. i. 11 there is no *Θεοῦ*, and both *τοῦ Κυρίου* and *σωτῆρος* refer to Jesus Christ. Winer pp. 154, 162. For 'our God' see above on *v.* 11.

ii. 1-17. DOCTRINAL AND HORTATORY

It has been pointed out that a pious expression of thanks to heaven was common, even in secular correspondence, as a prelude to the special subject of a letter, and that a more solemn and purposeful Thanksgiving is a general feature at the beginning of the Epistles of St. Paul. His Thanksgivings sometimes blossom out into a variety of subjects, as thoughts occur to him, but such subjects cannot be detached from the Thanksgiving; and not until the whole is completed are the subjects which are the reason for writing reached. In both of these letters to the Thessalonians the chief object of the writers is found in the second chapter, immediately after the prolonged Thanksgiving; and in both letters the development of the Thanksgiving forms an introduction to the leading topic which follows in the second chapter. In the First Epistle one of the chief objects was *to show the character and conduct of the writers during the work of converting the Thessalonians*; in this Epistle the chief object of the writers is *to explain their own teaching, and correct the ideas of the Thessalonians, respecting the Coming of Christ.* But although the *position* of this chapter is parallel to the *position* of the second chapter in the earlier letter, the *topic* of which it treats is parallel to that in the last chapter in the earlier letter, viz. the Time of the Coming of the Lord in that Day. A great deal must happen first.* The three missionaries had said so much about the duty of preparing for the Coming that the converts had concluded that it would happen almost at once; and this belief, so far from sobering all of them, and making them very circumspect in their conduct, had excited many of them, and made them think that it was not worth while to follow any regular course of life. These errors had to be corrected; but the method of correcting the misapprehension as to the Coming being immediate is surprising. Like the Lord's 'abomination of desolation standing where he ought not' (Mk. xiv. 13), it is cryptic; and, unlike that Saying, it is elaborate, consisting of a number of details, each of which is difficult for *us* to explain. The result is a passage which is very unlike anything else in the Pauline Epistles. Per-

* That a catastrophe of incalculable intensity was impending, and would be preceded by portents, was a common belief at this period; Suet., *Nero*, 36, 39; Tac., *Hist.* i. 3; *Ann.* xii. 43, 64, xiv. 12, 22, xv. 22. Renan, *L'Antechrist*, p. 35.

haps the nearest approach to it is 1 Cor. xv. 23–28; but the difference between the two passages is great, and the resemblance is small. Rev. xiii. would be nearer to it as a series of symbolical hints. Owing to the oral teaching which the Thessalonians had received, language which is very perplexing to us would be intelligible enough to them: in 2 Corinthians there is a great deal of detail that is of a similar character.

These remarks apply chiefly to the first twelve verses. The remaining two sections of the chapter, 13–15 and 16, 17, are free from the difficulties just mentioned; they are concerned with Thanksgiving leading on to Exhortation, and with Prayer. The second chapter, like the first and third, ends with Prayer.

ii. 1–12. Doctrine concerning the Time of the Lord's Coming

The Revelation of the Lawless One

We divide the perplexing paragraph into three sections. The first four verses are an earnest appeal to the Thessalonian Christians to refuse to listen to any teaching—from whatever source it may seem to come—which asserts that the Day of the Lord has already arrived. The Lawless One must first be revealed. The next three verses (5–7) correct the misunderstanding which has arisen respecting the Apostle's own teaching on the subject; the remaining five (8–12) declare the terrible end of the Lawless One.

ii. 1–4. *The Day of the Lord is not already Dawning.*

These verses introduce the second and main part of the Pauline Apocalypse. With regard to the uncertainty of the time of the Advent, which is as great now as it was in the first century, we may say with Augustine, *Ergo latet ultimus dies, ut observentur omnes dies.*

1 Now we beseech you, brethren, by the coming of our Lord Jesus Christ, and by our gathering together unto him, 2 That ye be not soon shaken in mind, or be troubled, neither by spirit, nor by word, nor by letter, as from us, as that the day of Christ is at hand. 3 Let

no man deceive you by any means, for *that day shall not come*, except there come a falling away first, and that man of sin be revealed, the son of perdition, [4] Who opposeth and exalteth himself above all that is called God, or that is worshipped: so that he as God, sitteth in the Temple of God, shewing himself that he is God.

Kennedy (*Last Things*, pp. 55 f., 167 f.) regards Mt. xxiv. as "the most instructive commentary" on these verses. He compares ii. 1 with Mt. xxiv. 31; ii. 2 with Mt. xxiv. 6; ii. 3 with Mt. xxiv. 12, 4; ii. 4 with Mt. xxiv. 15. It is probable that the Apostle was familiar, not with our Gospels, which were not yet written, but with the tradition of what Christ had said. At a time when all Christians believed that the Return was imminent, what He had said on the subject would frequently be repeated with more or less accuracy, and would be a conspicuous topic in the preaching of the first teachers. It is probable that this tradition had become somewhat confused, words which had referred to the destruction of Jerusalem becoming mixed with those which referred to the Last Day, before any of our Gospels were written. St. Paul would learn this tradition from some of the Twelve and possibly from others. His own words here are more full of meaning than a perusal of them in an English Version would lead one to suppose.

[1] We must now turn to the difficult subject to which our Thanksgiving has led us, respecting the Coming of our Lord Jesus in glory to inaugurate the great Day in which we, the persecuted saints, shall be gathered together to be united with Him. Accordingly as old friends we entreat you, Brethren, in the interests of truth respecting that Coming, [2] not to allow yourselves to be hastily driven from the safe anchorage of sober sense and sanity, nor yet—if you have for a time lost your bearings—to allow yourselves to be permanently disturbed, no matter what the apparent authority of the disturbing force may be,—whether some spiritual revelation, or statement of what we are reported to have said, or the production of a letter said to have come from us, to the effect that the Day of the Lord is already here. [3] Do not let any one so entirely deceive you by these or any other methods. Because the Coming will certainly not take place until the great Apostasy has preceded, and until there has been a revelation of the Man of Lawlessness, the inheritor of inevitable perdition. [4] He will prove to be the great adversary, exalting himself exceedingly against

every one that bears the name of God, or that is an object of worship, proclaiming himself to the world and saying that he really is God.

1. **We must now turn**] This is the effect of the connecting particle δέ, which implies both connexion and contrast with what has just been said; less connexion than 'and' (καί) and less contrast than but (ἀλλά). Each of the three words 'now,' 'and,' and 'but' must at different times be used according to the context. In 2 Thess. (ii. 1, 13, iii. 3, 4, 6, 12, 13, 14, 16), as in 1 Thess (ii. 16, 17, iii. 6, 11, 12, etc.), δέ is very frequent.

respecting the Coming etc.] It is quite certain that the A.V. is wrong in translating 'by the coming' and connecting this with 'we beseech you.' In this it is led astray by the Vulgate, *Rogamus autem vos, fratres, per adventum Domini.* The Greek (ὑπὲρ τῆς παρουσίας) cannot be an adjuration; and it is unlikely that the Parousia would be used as material for an adjuration. The preposition combines the idea of 'concerning' or 'respecting' with that of 'on behalf of,' *i.e.* in the interests of the truth respecting it, or stating the truth concerning it. Cf. παρακαλέσαι ὑπέρ 1 Thess. iii. 2. Winer, p. 479. Wetstein quotes *Aen.* i. 750, *Multa* super *Priamo rogitans,* super *Hectore multa.*

we shall be gathered together to be united with Him] Lit. '*our* gathering together up to Him.'* The double compound (ἐπισυναγωγή) is a substantive derived from the verb (ἐπισυνάγω) which is used by the Synoptists (Mk. xiii. 27; Mt. xxiv. 31) of the gathering together of the elect at the Lord's Coming. See also Lk. xiii. 34 of Christ's gathering the children of Jerusalem together. The substantive may have come to have a definite meaning in connexion with the Parousia. In 2 Macc. ii. 7 it is used of the idea which was

* 'Our' comes first with emphasis; our movement is contrasted with His. This reunion with Him is a frequent thought; 1 Thess. iv. 17, v. 10; 2 Cor. v. 8; Phil. i. 23: *cavendum ne quis excidat* (Bengel). That the reunion will come soon is also a frequent thought; Phil. iv. 5; Heb. x. 25, 37; 1 Pet. iv. 7; Jas. v. 8; 1 Jn. ii. 18.

current among the Jews after the return from the Captivity, that God would 'gather His people again together' from the lands of the Dispersion and greatly increase the population of Judaea. Cf. 2 Macc. i. 27; Zech. viii. 7, 8, x. 10; Heb. x. 25. So also in the Testaments of the XII. Patriarchs, *Naphtali* viii. 3, "For through their tribes shall God appear on earth to save Israel, and He shall gather together (ἐπισυνάξει) righteous ones from the Gentiles. Deissmann, *Light from the Ancient East*, pp. 101 f., illustrates ἐπισυναγώγη in the general signification of 'collection.'" The word is rare. Rutherford has 'our summons to muster before Him.'

as old friends we entreat you] The verb (ἐρωτῶμεν) in class. Grk. never means 'ask a favour,' but always 'ask a question.' But a request often takes the form of a question, as "Will you do this for me?" Thus the transition from the earlier use to the later is easy. Both uses are frequent in N.T., especially in Lk. and Jn. St. Paul has the verb four times; here, 1 Thess. iv. 1, v. 12, and Phil iv. 3,—always in the sense of 'entreat,' 'request.' As distinct from other verbs which mean 'entreat,' it implies familiarity and equality with the person or persons addressed. The writers put themselves on a level with their converts. They are not commanding or exhorting as superiors (iii. 4, 6 10, 12), but entreating as friends. The addition of 'Brethren,' (i. 3) is again a mark of affectionate regard.

2. **not to allow**] With εἰς τό here cf. 1 Thess. ii. 12, iii. 10.

hastily] The Thessalonians had readily and suddenly (ταχέως) adopted this erroneous opinion, without giving themselves time to consider; the position had been rushed. Cf. 'Lay hands suddenly (ταχέως) on no man,' 1 Tim. v. 22; 'I marvel that ye are so quickly (ταχέως) removing,' Gal. i. 6. 'Be not readily set adrift' (Rutherford).

driven from the safe anchorage] The verb (σαλευθῆναι) is used of ships being forced from their moorings by the pressure of a storm, and in the LXX it is frequent of the movement produced by wind and weather; also in the N.T., Mt. xi. 7; Lk. vi. 48, vii. 24. It is also used, as here, in a figurative sense, *Οὐ μὴ σαλευθῶ*, Ps. ix. 27 (x. 6), xxix. (xxx. 7). Cf. Acts xvii. 13 of the Thessalonian Jews driving the multitude at Beroea to hostility; and Epictetus, *Diss.* iii. 26 *μὴ ἀποσαλεύεσθαι διὰ σοφισμάτων*: also, Judith xii. 16; Ecclus. xiii. 21.

from . . . sober sense and sanity] 'Shaken *in* mind' (A.V.) is certainly wrong; 'shaken *from* your mind' (R.V.) is the meaning of *σαλευθῆναι ὑμᾶς ἀπὸ τοῦ νοός*. The aorist indicates the definite shock; and we have *ἀπό* in a similar sense i. 9. 'Mind' means their normal, sober state of mind, *quae in sana doctrina acquiescit* (Calvin). They are not to allow themselves to be 'swung round by any wind of doctrine' (Eph. iv. 14), so as to lose their mental balance. *Νοῦς* is frequent in Paul, but is rare elsewhere in N.T. On the form *νοός* see A. T. Robertson, *Gr.* p. 261.

nor yet to allow yourselves to be permanently disturbed] To be startled by what they were told might be unavoidable; but they must not give way and suffer themselves 'to be troubled.' Cf. Mk. xiii. 7 and Mt. xxiv. 6, where the same verb (*θροεῖσθαι*) is used of the same kind of trouble. St. Paul may have had the Saying in his mind. In all three places we have the present tense of continued emotion. This 'troubling' might be true of those who looked forward to the Second Coming with dread, as well as of those who looked forward to it with intense longing. For 'nor yet' (*μηδέ*) cf. Rom. xiv. 21; for *θροεῖσθαι* see Kennedy, *Sources of N.T. Greek*, p. 126; for *μηδὲ . . . μήτε*, Winer, p. 618.

whether some spiritual revelation] Here we come upon a series of brief expressions which the Thessalonians would understand, but at the meaning of which we can only guess. Three agencies which were possibly instrumental in producing unhealthy excitement are mentioned, 'spirit,' 'word,' and 'letter'; after which come the words 'as from us,' implying that there had been, or it was feared that there might have been, the production of evidence, in which the Apostle and his colleagues were represented as having stated that the Day of the Lord had come. All such representations were false. It is clear that 'as from us' must apply to the 'letter'; the writers think that there *may* have been a forged epistle. Is 'as from us' to be confined to the letter? The R.V. implies this, for it omits the comma after 'by epistle.' It is difficult to believe that there is not close connexion between 'by word' and 'by epistle,' the one referring to a verbal statement attributed to the missionaries, the other to a written letter attributed to them. In that case 'as from us' must be extended to 'by word.' But if that extension is admitted, must not 'as from us' apply to 'by spirit' also? Yet St. Paul makes such abrupt changes, as ideas occur to him while he is dictating, that it is possible that 'as from us' was not in his mind when he said 'by spirit.' Each of the three interpretations is tenable; but on the whole it seems best to confine 'as by us' to 'by word' and 'by letter.' That it belongs to both of these seems probable from ii. 15. With διά here cf. 1 Cor. xiv. 9; 2 Cor. vi. 7; 3 Jn. 13.

'By spirit' (διὰ πνεύματος) probably refers either to *ecstatic* utterance by some who were believed to have the gift of speaking in a Tongue, or to *inspired* utterance by some who were believed to have the gift of Prophecy. Both of these gifts were common in the Church of Corinth, and they may have been common at Thessalonica (1 Thess. v. 19). It is possible that some ecstatic utterance had been interpreted to mean that the great Day had dawned, or preachers who claimed to be inspired had declared that this was so. Theodore understands it to mean a false prophet. A gift for the discerning of spirits was a necessary charisma in the primitive Church.

If 'as from us' is carried back to this first suggestion, the meaning will be that the advocates of the erroneous teaching appealed to a revelation which they said had been made by the Apostle or his companions. In any case the ὡς gives the statement a subjective character. Winer, p. 770.

what we are reported to have said] 'By word' (διὰ λόγου) might refer to misinterpretation of what the missionaries had said or (more probably) to invention of things which they had not said. In any case it means intelligible discourse, and not ecstatic utterance.

a letter said to have come from us] That there had been error is stated, and that there had been deception is implied; but we are not sure as to the manner of the supposed deception. The brevity and indefiniteness of the expression might suggest that the writers had grave suspicions, but were not quite certain about the facts. Are they alluding to 1 *Thessalonians*, which the Apostle solemnly charged the recipients to have read 'to *all* the brethren,' that there might be no doubt as to the exact language used (v. 27)? Possibly this had not been properly done, and what had been written respecting the Coming had been misrepresented, *e.g.* ἐφίσταται (v. 3) interpreted as ἐνέστηκεν. This explanation is adopted by Paley, *Horae Paulinae*, X. iii. 3, 4. But it is scarcely in harmony with the text, which says that the epistle itself was in question rather than the meaning of certain passages in it. No explanation of misunderstood passages is here given, such as we have in 1 Cor. v. 9, 10.

There is no need to debate whether here there is allusion to a *letter which has been lost*; of any such letter from the Apostle to the Thessalonians there is no trace. The alternative to the First Epistle is *suspicion of a forged letter*; and of the existence of such a suspicion there seems to be evidence in iii. 17, where St. Paul says that in this and future letters the final salutation in his own handwriting is to be a sign of authenticity. He suspects that a letter as from him to the Thessalonians has been, or might be, forged. Of course it is possible that he *knew* that there was such a letter. But it is somewhat improbable that, while he was still in touch with the Thessalonians, any person would venture on such a device. On the other hand, when doctrine was openly attributed to him which he knew that he had never taught, he might wonder whether people could be making use of a forged letter. This touch is against 2 Thessalonians being itself a forgery. In Gal. i. 8, 9 we have a similar protestation.

to the effect that] The same expression (ὡς ὅτι) occurs 2 Cor. v. 19, xi. 21. In xi. 21, as here, it helps to suggest that the statement is not worthy of credit; in v. 19 it does not do so, and indeed differs little from ὅτι without ὡς. Here the statement is discredited by the context; and ὡς, 'to the effect' or 'representing' agrees well with what is quoted as a misstatement. See on 1 Thess. v. 1, 2; also A.T. Robertson, *Gr.*, p. 1033.

the Day of the Lord] The A.V. has 'Christ' for 'the Lord,' following late authorities; the oldest and best are decisive for 'the Lord' (R.V.).

is already here] Here again the A.V. is at fault, not through following a corrupt reading, but through a mistranslation which mars the sense. The Apostle himself believed that the Day 'is at hand' (A.V.), and he would not have criticized so severely those who merely quoted this belief as certainly true. 'Is at hand' might be ἤγγικεν (Rom. xiii. 2) or ἐγγύς ἐστιν (Phil. iv. 5). The erroneous teachers declared that the Day 'is now present' (R.V.); the time is already come. The verb (ἐνέστηκεν, perfect, with present meaning) means more than 'is at hand' or 'is imminent.' The Lord had not yet manifested Himself in glory, but 'the Day' in which He would do so had begun, had 'set in.' Cf. 1 Cor. iii. 22, vii. 26; Gal. i. 4; Heb. ix. 9, where the perfect participle is used in the sense of being present; also Rom. viii. 38 and 1 Cor. iii. 22, where 'things present' (ἐνεστῶτα) are expressly contrasted with 'things to come' (μέλλοντα). In papyri the participle is used of the current year. 'The Day of the Lord' was not a solar day of twenty-four hours, but a period of time, and St. Paul contradicts the opinion that they were already living in that period. He believed that it was near, but he never taught this belief as a certainty, and he had never said that the Day had arrived.

There is no real difficulty about the fact that richly inspired persons were allowed for a time to hold the erroneous belief that the Lord would return soon. Acts i. 6, 7 is sufficient explanation of that. Even our Lord Himself, in the time of His humiliation, was ignorant on that point; Mk. xiii. 32; Mt. xxiv. 36 (R.V.).

3. **do not let any one so entirely deceive you**] This is a more explicit monition than *v.* 2. It states, not only that they have troubled themselves with an erroneous idea, but that there are deceitful teachers who have given them this idea. The compound ἐξαπατάω is more common in the N.T. than the simple ἀπατάω, and, excepting Jas. i. 26, both are confined to the Pauline Epistles. Warnings against such teachers are frequent; Rom. xvi. 18; 1 Cor. iii. 18; Eph. v. 6; Col. ii. 4, 8. In what follows here, 'by any means' (A.V.) is preferable to 'in any wise' (R.V.); not merely the means just mentioned, but any others which crafty teachers may devise; cf. 3 Macc. iv. 13; 4 Macc. iv. 24, x. 7. With μή τις and the 3rd. pers. aor. subj. cf. 1 Cor. xvi. 11; 2 Cor. xi. 16.

the Coming will certainly not take place] This is the obvious apodosis to the 'until' clause,—so obvious that St. Paul does not think it necessary to state it. But he may have intended to state it after that clause, and in dictating forgot to do so. Farrar thinks that he was unwilling to insert such discouraging words and purposely suppressed them. Cf. the unfinished sentence Rom. v. 12 and the broken sentences Gal. ii. 4–7. Winer, p. 749.

until the great Apostasy has preceded] Or, 'unless the great Apostasy come first.' The definite article, ἡ ἀποστασία, which is ignored in the A.V. ('*a* falling away'), implies two things; that 'the Apostasy' is a matter of importance, and that the Thessalonians know what it means. Winer, p. 132. Doubtless the Apostle had instructed them on the subject. It was a topic with which they were familiar; and therefore, unfortunately for us, he here gives little explanation. He had told them that there would be two comings, the coming of the Apostasy and the Coming of the Lord. The interval between the two might be brief, but the Apostasy would certainly precede. As this had not yet taken place, it was a serious error to declare that the Day of the Lord's Coming had arrived. Beet, *Last Things*,

p. 99. On the "supreme intensification of evil and sin" which the N.T. indicates as a sign that the end of the world is approaching, see Clemen, *Primitive Christianity*, pp. 117 f. Cf. 1 Cor. vii. 29; 2 Tim. iii. 1–9; Jude 17 f.; Rev. vi. 1 f.; viii. 7 f., xvi. 1 f.; 2 Esdras v. 1, 2; Enoch xci. 7–9.

What is meant by the Apostasy? The Greek word is a late and not very common form of ἀπόστασις, meaning 'defection,' 'revolt,' 'rebellion.' In the LXX and the N.T. (here and Acts xxi. 21) it means *religious* revolt, from the worship of God or the Law of Moses. Cf. Heb. iii. 12. Here revolt from God is evidently meant, and those who are guilty of it must be apostate Jews or apostate Christians. The heathen are 'unbelievers,' 'aliens,' 'outsiders' (1 Thess. iv. 12; 1 Cor. v. 12, 13; Col. iv. 5; 1 Tim. iii. 7), rather than apostates or revolters. *Apostasiam vocat Paulus perfidam a Deo defectionem* (Calvin). *Apostasia est defectio a fide, dilucideque describitur*, 1 Tim. iv. 1 (Bengel) Cf. The Testaments of the XII Patriarchs, *Dan.* v. 4, 5. This consideration clears the ground for us when we come to consider what is meant by 'the Man of Lawlessness.'

The Latins are not agreed as to the rendering of ἀποστασία. Tertullian has *abscessio*, the Vulgate *discessio*, Ambrosiaster *defectio*. Augustine makes it equivalent to ἀποστάτης and has *refuga*: like Chrysostom and other Greek Fathers, he regards it as abstract for concrete. But we cannot safely identify Antichrist with the Apostasy; he seems rather to be the chief outcome and promoter of it.

As we might suppose, our Lord's prediction of a great apostasy (Mk. xiii. 21–23; Mt. xxiv. 10–12, 23, 24) made a great impression on the first generation of Christians. Briggs, *The Messiah of the Gospels*, pp. 143, 147. The discourse in which it occurs seems to have been familiar to St. Paul and to have been much in his mind while he was dictating these two letters. Cf. also Rom. xvi. 17, 18; Eph. iv. 14; 1 Tim. iv. 1–3; 2 Tim. iii. 1–8, iv. 3, 4; Acts xx. 29. The Johannine Books exhibit similar features. We are not surprised, therefore, to find that St. Paul and his colleagues had implanted these ideas in the minds of the Thessalonians.

until there has been a revelation] This impressive word (ἀποκαλυφθῇ) is placed first with emphasis, and may be kept in front in translation. Its importance is shown by its repetition in *vv.* 6 and 8. But there is nothing in the construction to show whether we have two events which are to precede the Coming of the Lord Jesus, or only one; whether this 'revelation' is an additional fact, or only the great Apostasy described in detail. In any case two revelations seem to be placed in strong contrast,—a revelation of immense and mysterious wickedness, and a revelation of immense and mysterious glory; and the latter will vanquish and consume the former, which must precede it (i. 7–10, ii. 8). Revelation implies mystery beyond human experience. See Hastings' *D.C.G.* art. 'Revelation.'

the Man of Lawlessness] The reading is somewhat uncertain. The two best uncials, with ten cursives, three important versions, and two Latin Fathers support 'lawlessness' (ἀνομίας), and their authority seems to outweigh that of the majority of witnesses, which have 'sin' (ἁμαρτίας). R.V., however, has the latter. If *vv.* 7, 8 had *preceded* this one, we might have supposed that an early copyist had changed ἁμαρτίας to ἀνομίας to agree with ἄνομος there. But such a change would be less likely in the existing arrangement; and the witness of Tertullian and Ambrose considerably weakens the witness of the Latin versions. In 1 Jn. iii. 4 sin is declared to be lawlessness and lawlessness to be sin; seeing that both words have the article, ἡ ἁμαρτία ἐστὶν ἡ ἀνομία, the two terms are convertible. Everywhere in N.T. ἀνομία, like 'lawlessness,' means not mere absence of law, but violation of it, conscious and wilful disregard of it, and such disregard is sin. As regards meaning, therefore, it makes little difference which reading we adopt. In LXX ἀνομία very often represents the Hebrew for 'abomination,' and in Hebrew 'the man of abomination' might mean one who claimed worship as an idol. E. A. Abbott, *The Son of Man*, p. 347. '*The* man' (R.V.)

is right; '*that* man' (A.V.) is another exaggeration of the Greek article; see on i. 11. Cf. 'man of war' Exod. xv. 3; Josh. xvii. 1; 1 Sam. xvi. 18; 'man of Belial' (worthlessness) 2 Sam. xvi. 7, xx. 1; 'man of blood' 2 Sam. xvi. 7; etc. Winer, p. 298.

This mysterious figure is a new development. It is connected with the false Christs predicted by our Lord, but it is based on the Antichrist of Jewish apocalyptic, especially on Daniel. It is remarkable that the LXX renders the obscure word 'Belial' by *ἀνομία*, 2 Sam. xxii. 5, by *ἀνόμημα*, Deut. xv. 9, and by *ἀποστασία*, 1 Kings xxi. 13 (3 Kings xx. 13 A text). Aquila also has *ἀποστασία*, 1 Sam. ii. 12, x. 27, xxv. 17. This is in favour of identifying the Man of Lawlessness with Belial or Beliar. See *Enc. Bibl.*, art. 'Belial.' No recorded words of Christ tell of a single individual as a consummate opponent to the Messiah and to all that is good. St. Paul intimates that this last false Christ will be welcomed, not only by the heathen, but by the majority of the Jews. Christians must be prepared for this. It will be well to consider other details in the description of this appalling being before trying to arrive at any conclusion as to who or what is meant by the description.

the inheritor of inevitable perdition] This, like 'man of lawlessness,' is a Hebraistic mode of expression, in which the genitive of a substantive takes the place of an adjective. It is specially common with 'son' or 'sons'; *e.g.* 'sons of thunder' Mk. iii. 17; 'son of peace' Lk. x. 6; 'sons of light' Lk. xvi. 8; Jn. xii. 36; 'son of perdition' Jn. xvii. 12. Cf. Eph. ii. 2, v. 6, and see on 1 Thess. v. 5. While 'man of lawlessness' indicates his character, 'son of perdition,' *υἱὸς τῆς ἀπωλείας*, shows what is certain to be his end. It does not mean that he will be the cause of perdition to others; that he 'exists to destroy'; that would be 'father of perdition'; cf. Jn. viii. 44. Judas is called 'the son of perdition,' of whom it is said that he fell away from his apostleship, 'that he might go to his own place' Acts. i. 25. Cf. 'son of Gehenna' Mt. xxiii. 15; 'son of stripes' Deut. xxv. 2; 'son of death' 1 Sam. xx. 31 (R.V. marg.). The nature of the subject has led St. Paul to adopt the language and symbolism of Hebrew prophecy and apocalypse. In the Book of Jubilees x. 3 those who perished in the Deluge are 'sons of perdition'; Noah and his family were saved, and they were lost. In Rev. xvii. 11 the Beast (Antichrist) 'goes into perdition.'

4. **the great adversary**] The opponent of Christ and His Gospel, Antichrist. *Ut Antichristum cognoscas, Christum ex diametro illi opponere convenit* (Calvin). Certainly Satan is not meant, as is clear from *v.* 9; but, as Chrysostom remarks, Satan inspires him with his own persistent activity and astuteness. Possibly a parallel is meant between this indwelling of Satan and the Incarnation (Theod. Mops.). Some identify the Lawless one with Beliar or Belial, and Charles regards this as almost certain (*Asc. Isaiah*, lxi. f.). So also do Bousset (*Der Antichrist*; Eng. tr. *The Antichrist Legend*) and Friedländer. See Kennedy, *St. Paul's Conceptions of the Last Things*, p. 209. In the *Martyrdom of Isaiah* ii. 4 we have "For the angel of lawlessness, who is the ruler of this world, is Beliar." The problem admits of no sure solution. See Swete, *Revelation*, pp. lxxv. f.; Thackeray, *Relation of St. Paul to Contemporary Jewish Thought*, pp. 136 f.

exalting himself exceedingly] Another compound of ὑπέρ: see on i. 3. Elsewhere in N.T. ὑπεραίρομαι occurs only 2 Cor. xii. 7.

against every one] This, rather than 'above all' (A.V.), is the meaning of ἐπὶ πάντα. The A.V. is here again misled by the Vulgate, *supra omne quod dicitur Deus*. No doubt *supra* and 'above' partly represent the ὑπερ- in ὑπεραιρόμενος, but that means 'above measure,' 'exceedingly'; and πάντα is masculine, not neuter. Although the two participles have only one article, ἐπὶ πάντα belongs to ὑπεραιρόμενος alone, not to ἀντικείμενος also. Cf. *Homo supra mensuram humanae superbiae tumens* (Seneca, *De Benef.*, v. 6).

that bears the name of God] 'Though there be that are called gods' 1 Cor. viii. 5. In Daniel xi. 36, which the Apostle has in his mind, we have 'every god.' Here the heathen divinities are included, and 'every god,' without qualification, might seem to imply that the Christian God was only the highest among many. The Thessalonians had recently been polytheists, and the old ideas were still latent in some of them. 'That bears the name of' is confined to 'God'; it must not be carried on to 'an object of worship.' The heathen deities had the name of God without the reality, but their idols were really objects of worship. In spite of the change of gender, πάντα is to be carried on to σεβασμα: see on i. 11. Σέβασμα occurs elsewhere in N.T. Acts xvii. 23 only, and there in the plural, which the A.V. wrongly renders 'devotions.' It is correctly rendered Wisd. xv. 17, where the idolater is said to be 'better than the things which he worshippeth,' κρείττων τῶν σεβασμάτων αὐτοῦ. Bengel suggests an allusion to ὁ Σεβαστός, the Roman Emperor (Acts xxv. 21), which is not probable. Here Vulg. has *quod colitur*, Acts xvii. 23 *simulacra*.

so that he even dares to seat himself] This is the result actually reached by him, ὥστε αὐτὸν . . . καθίσαι. We have a similar construction with a similar consecutive force 1 Thess. i. 7. This is what his exalting himself ends in. As generally in N.T., καθίσαι is here intransitive; but 1 Cor. vi. 4 and Eph. i. 20 are exceptions, and Jn. xix. 13 is doubtful. The R.V. rightly omits 'as God' (A.V.); the words are a gloss inserted in later and inferior authorities; but Chrys. and Theodt. had it.

in the sanctuary of God] Literally '*into* the sanctuary,' εἰς τὸν ναόν. He goes into it and seats himself there. We often have εἰς with a verb of rest; Mk. x. 10, xiii. 16; Lk. xi. 7, xxi. 37; Acts viii. 40; etc.; and conversely ἐν after a verb of motion; Mt. x. 16; Lk. ix. 46, x. 3; thus both motion and the subsequent rest are expressed concisely. Winer, p. 514. In late Greek the difference between εἰς and ἐν becomes somewhat blurred. Blass, *Gram.*, §39, 3. The 'sanctuary' (ναός) is that part of the 'Temple' (ἱερόν) into which the priests alone entered. It was roofed, whereas much of the Temple consisted of open courts. Excepting 1 Cor. ix. 13, St. Paul never uses ἱερόν, and where he uses *ναός*, 'the sanctuary of God,' the meaning is figurative; 1 Cor. iii. 16–19; 2 Cor. vi. 16; Eph. ii. 21. The meaning is probably figurative here. We often have 'sitting' used in a figurative sense; Col. iii. 1; Heb. i. 3, viii. 1, x. 12, xii. 2; Rev. iii. 21, xx. 4. We must bear in mind that the Apostle is alluding to what the Thessalonians had previously been taught; and he had of course taught them that a Christian congregation, and indeed every Christian soul, is a sanctuary of God. He is not here asserting that this adversary will actually enter the sanctuary of the Jewish Temple or any Christian building. He is saying that this adversary will claim the highest honours which man pays to God. It is possible that the attempt of the mad Caligula to get his own image set up in the Temple at Jerusalem, some ten or twelve years before the date of this Epistle, viz., A.D. 40, may have suggested this figure of speech.* Chrysostom, Theodoret, and Theodore of Mopsuestia interpret figuratively, and this is generally the modern view; but Milligan follows Irenaeus in adopting a literal reference. Only if the Man of Lawlessness is a person, and not a principle personified, can the literal view be held. Moreover, if the person is regarded as a false Messiah, all reference to Caligula or Nero is excluded. "We are not to imagine a person suddenly coming forward and claiming divine honours. The Apostle is speaking of a form of evil springing out of the state of the world itself, to which mankind are ready to give homage" (Jowett).

proclaiming himself to the world] Literally 'showing himself off,' *ἀποδεικνύντα ἑαυτόν*. The verb is also used of

* Philo, *Legatio ad Caium*, § 16, M. 562, tells how the whole world, men, women, cities, nations, flattered Caligula and increased his inordinate pride. The Jews alone refused to take any part in the blasphemy of making a mortal man into an eternal God. But he would allow nothing on earth, not even this one Temple, left to God the Lord, but insisted that everywhere his own divinity should be worshipped. In reply to the deputation of Alexandrian Jews he used words of blasphemy, which even to listen to, Philo says, was sin. See Lewin, *Fasti Sacri*, A.D. 40.

appointing or nominating a person to be a general or other official. It is also used of proclaiming a king on his accession; so in Josephus and Philo. Wetstein gives illustrations. Any one of these three meanings makes good sense here.

Contrast what is said of Christ, Acts ii. 22, that He is ἀποδεδειγμένον ἀπὸ τοῦ Θεοῦ. Cf. the *Ascension of Isaiah* iv. 6, where we read of Beliar that "he [will do and] will speak like the Beloved, and he will say, It is I who am the Lord, and before me there was none" (Tisseraut, p. 118).

that he really is God] The ἔστιν is emphatic. His proclamation of himself is actually to that effect. It is possible that the deification of the Roman Emperor may have suggested this detail, but the passage in Daniel would suffice, without further suggestion; and that Daniel is in the Apostle's mind is beyond a doubt, when his words and Dan. xi. 36, 37 are placed side by side. But we must not think that the interpretation of Daniel's words will help us to interpret the language of St. Paul. While the picturesque imagery remains the same, because it is the traditional vehicle of prophetic and apocalyptic utterance, it may be a very misleading guide as to interpretation. We must interpret St. Paul, not by what O.T. Prophets meant when they used similar language, but by what he himself meant in other places in which he describes the present features and immediate prospects of his own age. Jowett, I. pp. 182–188. On Rev. xiii. 6 Charles quotes the *Ascension of Isaiah* iv. 6 (before 100 A.D.), "He will say; I am God, and before me there has been none": the *Sibylline Oracles,* v. 33, 34 (before 130 A.D.), "Then he shall return, making himself equal to God." Of Caligula Philo writes (*Leg. ad Caium* 23), "Not merely saying, but also thinking, that he is God."

The R.V. is used in making this comparison between Daniel and St. Paul. See also p. xviii.

Daniel xi. 36, 37.	2 *Thess.* ii. 3–12.
The king shall do according to his will; and he shall exalt himself, and magnify himself above every god, and shall speak marvellous things against the God of gods; and he shall prosper till the indignation be accomplished; for that which is determined shall be done. Neither shall he regard the gods of his fathers, nor regard any god: for he shall magnify himself above all.	The man of lawlessness, he that opposeth and exalteth himself against all that is called God or that is worshipped; so that he sitteth in the temple of God, setting himself forth as God, the son of perdition, whom the Lord shall slay and destroy. And exalteth himself against all that is called God or that is worshipped; setting himself forth as God.

The prophecy in Daniel refers primarily, and perhaps exclusively, to Antiochus Epiphanes, who assumed divine honours, as his later coins show: see Driver *ad loc.* Antiochus may be regarded as a *type* of Antichrist; but there is no doubt that these two verses, like those which precede them (21–35) refer to Antiochus. There is no abrupt change of reference.

It will be worth while to look also at Dan. vii. 25, 26 and compare what is said there with some of the Apostle's words. He may have had that passage also in his mind.

Daniel vii. 25, 26.	2 Thess. ii. 3–12.
He shall speak words against the Most High and he shall think to change the times and the law. But the judgment shall sit, and they shall take away his dominion, to consume and to destroy it unto the end.	he that opposeth and exalteth himself against God. the lawless one. that they all might be judged, the son of perdition, whom the Lord Jesus shall slay and destroy.

The person to whom this passage in Daniel refers is a matter that is greatly disputed, but it need not be discussed here. All that concerns us is to consider whether the language in Daniel has influenced the language in our Epistle. That Dan. xi. 36, 37 has done so is beyond doubt; and this earlier passage may have done so also. See Garrod *ad loc.*, who makes the above comparisons.

The first section of this second chapter ends very abruptly. Winer, p. 749.

ii. 5–7. *Reminder respecting the Apostle's Oral Teaching.*

The Apostle seems to feel that he need not continue these details, with which the Thessalonians have been made familiar. He breaks off suddenly and appeals to their recollection of his words. Cf. the appeal in 1 Thess. ii. 9. Here, however, his language is so allusive, that, although the Thessalonians doubtless understood it, we are reduced to guessing; and we cannot be certain that any one of the various conjectures is correct.

[5] Remember ye not, that when I was yet with you, I told you these things? [6] And now ye know what withholdeth, that he might be revealed in his time. [7] For the mystery of iniquity doth already work: only he who now letteth, will let, until he be taken out of the way.

Like our Lord (Mk. viii. 18; Jn. xiv. 9, xv. 20), the Apostle appeals to the experience which his converts have had of his teaching. Cf. Acts xx. 31. The words are a gentle rebuke; they ought to have remembered. The subject was so important, and the time since they were told about it was so short. Cf. Acts xx. 31 and the rebuke to the Corinthians for forcing him to praise himself 2 Cor. xii. 11.

[5] You surely must remember, how that, while I was still living among you, I used habitually to instruct you respecting the Coming of the Lord Jesus on the great Day, and used to tell you how that the Lawless One must appear first. [6] And for the present time, you already

know from your own experience the power which restrains him from appearing, so that he may not be fully revealed until the season divinely appointed to him for *his* revelation has arrived. [7] I say fully revealed rather tham come into existence, for, as a matter of fact, this mysterious principle of lawlessness is already set to do its evil work ; only it does this work in secret, without being revealed, until he who for the present is restraining it from appearing be taken out of the way.

5. **You surely must remember**] The verb (*μνημονεύω*) in St. Paul always means ' remember ' (1 Thess. i. 3, ii. 9 ; Gal. ii. 10 ; Eph. ii. 11 ; Col. iv. 18), and never ' make mention of ' or ' remind ' (Heb. xi. 22). So also generally in LXX. St. John in like manner reminds his little children that they have already been instructed about the coming of Antichrist. " The subject formed part of the general apostolic teaching " (Brooke on 1 Jn. ii. 18).

while I was still living among you] Or, ' when I was at home with you ' (*πρὸς ὑμᾶς*) ; cf. iii. 10 ; 1 Thess. iii. 4 ; 1 Cor. xvi. 7 ; Gal. i. 18 ; Philem. 13 ; etc.

I used habitually] Imperfect tense (*ἔλεγον*) ; oral instruction is evidently meant. It is not the brief and somewhat indistinct teaching given in the First Epistle (iv. 13–18, v. 1–11) that is alluded to here. He had given them full and clear instruction about these matters by word of mouth. In 1 Thess. v. 2 he says that they ' know perfectly ' about the Day of the Lord, and this implies much previous teaching : the hostile Jews knew that he taught that Jesus is alive and reigning (Acts xvii. 7). It is evident that the coming of the Lawless One was a leading topic in his preaching ; he had told them of the existing signs of his appearing and of the cause of his delay.

Here for the first and only time, until just at the end (iii. 17), does St. Paul use the 1st person singular. He does not appeal to what his colleagues have done. But he knows very well what he said himself ; and he spoke so frequently and fully on these subjects that the Thessalonians ought not to have allowed themselves to be so entirely misled by other teachers. Contrast ' *we* say ' 1 Thess. iv. 15.

6. **And for the present time**] There is some uncertainty as to how the two Greek words (καὶ νῦν) should be rendered. We have choice of three interpretations. The words are possibly *argumentative* ; 'I taught you : *well then,* your own experience has confirmed the teaching.' 'Well then' would mean 'to pass on to a further point.' This argumentative νῦν is frequent in 1 Cor. (v. 11, vii. 14, xii. 18, 20, xiv. 6), but always νῦν δέ, not καὶ νῦν. And we have this argumentative νῦν with 'know' following, Acts. iii. 17. See also Acts iii. 17, x. 5, xiii. 11, xx. 25, xxii. 16 ; 1 Jn. ii. 28 ; 2 Jn. 5. But 'And now' may also be *temporal,* and that in two ways. It may refer to the time of writing in contrast to the time when he was with them ; 'I taught you a great deal then ; *and now* your own experience has taught you more.' But (perhaps best of all) it may refer to the time of writing in contrast to the appointed season which is yet to come. Some commentators suggest taking νῦν with τὸ κάτεχον, 'that which at present restrains' ; but this would require τὸ νῦν κάτεχον.

you already know] This must not be watered down into meaning 'you know what *is* the power which restrains,' or 'you know something *about* the power.' It means that the Thessalonians have personal acquaintance with it ; they have had experience of its operation, and they will understand what is meant. In subjects such as these, cryptic expressions are usual ; and to speak more plainly might in this case be dangerous, for the power which restrains would resent the prediction that it is to be taken out of the way. Hence the indefinite expression, neuter here and masculine in the next verse. Cf. Lk. i. 35, where we have first the neuter participle and then a masculine substantive of the unborn Christ.

the power which restrains] 'The withholding thing,' 'that which holds fast' and keeps in check the Lawless One, so that he cannot as yet be fully revealed. Cf. Lk. iv. 42, where the same verb (κατέχω) is used in the same sense. 'Holding fast' may have two very different purposes ; to prevent a precious thing from being lost or injured, and to prevent a dangerous thing from doing harm. We have the one idea 1 Thess. v. 21 and 1 Cor. xi. 2, the other here. It is not likely that the Apostle means 'that which prevents me from speaking plainly.'

so that he may not be fully revealed] This is the end or purpose which Providence has in view in causing the restraining power to keep the great Adversary for the present in check. We have the same construction (εἰς τό with the infinitive) *v.* 11 and 1 Thess. ii. 12. The Thessalonians do not as yet know the Lawless One, although they have felt some of the effects of his baleful activity; but they do know the power which restrains him from being manifested in all his terrible characteristics.

until the season for his revelation has arrived] The Man of Lawlessness has *his* season (ἐν τῷ αὐτοῦ καιρῷ, 1 Thess. v. 1), appointed by the authority of the Father (Acts i. 7), and his hour is not yet come, although it is near. 'His' is emphatic by position. The hour of the Lord's Passion was an hour of Lawlessness, in which darkness got the upper hand. But a worse hour is impending (1 Tim. iv. 1; 2 Tim. iii. 1, iv. 3; 2 Pet. iii. 3; Jude 18 f.), of which the Apostle goes on to speak. For the present, however, God is using some earthly power to prevent the outburst of evil from being manifested before its time.

7. **for this mysterious principle is already set to do its evil work**] It is made to develop its malign energy. 'For' explains why the Apostle has used such an expression as 'revealed.' With him a 'mystery' is something which has been kept secret from mankind, until it pleased God to reveal it. Then it becomes a marvellous paradox,—a secret which everybody knows. 'Mystery' and 'revelation,' therefore, are with him closely related terms. If there has been a mystery, there has been, or will be, a revelation; and if there is never any revelation, it is futile to talk of a mystery; Rom. xvi. 25; 1 Cor. ii. 7, 10; Eph. iii. 3, 9, 10; Col. i. 26. 'For' (γάρ) is less frequent in this letter than in 1 Thess.; but, where it does occur, it is equally important to see what it implies, and this is shown in the

paraphrase, iii. 2, 7, 10, 11. 'Already' (ἤδη) is in contrast to the season appointed for the revelation, which has not yet come, but is believed to be near, as 'already' indicates.*

This shows that no real contradiction (as is sometimes asserted) between 1 and 2 Thessalonians can be said to exist. In both Epistles it is intimated that the Day of the Lord is near, and that the exact time is uncertain. In this Epistle additional information is given. Certain signs will precede the Day, and the signs have already begun to work. 'Set to do' is perhaps more accurate than 'is doing' or 'doth work,' for the verb (ἐνεργεῖται) is probably passive rather than middle (J. A. Robinson, *Ephesians*, pp. 246 f.). It is Satan who sets the evil influence in operation. Cf. 'There shall be delay no longer.' Rev. x. 6; see Swete and Charles *ad loc.* 'There shall be *time* no longer' is misleading.

only . . . until he who for the present is restraining it] The Greek sentence, like that in *v.* 3, seems to be somewhat incoherent, and we may supply what *appears* to be meant, but which St. Paul does not state. All that he gives us is 'only he who for the present is restraining, until he be taken out of the way.' We may supply 'is there' (R.V.) or 'is also at work,' which is less violent than 'will let' (A.V.). But with Alford, B. Weiss and others we need supply nothing; ὁ κατέχων ἄρτι is placed before ἕως ἐκ μέσου γένητα' for emphasis; 'only until he who now hinders is removed. See Lightfoot on Gal. ii. 10 and Plummer on 2 Cor. ii. 4, where we have similar inversions for the sake of emphasis. The general sense is the same, however we explain the construction. The evil is already secretly in operation, and he who is a check on its being made manifest is also

* In construction τῆς ἀνομίας is probably a genitive of apposition, and is an afterthought to define τὸ μυστήριον. On μυστήριον see Hatch, *Essays in Bibl. Grk.* pp. 57 f.; Lightfoot on Col. i. 26; J. A. Robinson, *Ephesians*, pp. 234 f. We must keep the word 'mystery' ('obscure force' or 'secret force' is no improvement) and 'the mystery' is by position very emphatic.

for the moment in operation : but the one who checks will be removed, and then the full manifestation of the evil will take place.

The A.V. is here very unsatisfactory. It has 'withholdeth' and then 'letteth,' the Greek verb being the same (κατέχω), and the same power or person being meant. The Vulgate has *quid detineat* and *qui tenet.* We have three different Greek words expressing different shades of meaning with regard to present time ; νῦν 'now,' ἤδη 'already,' and ἄρτι 'for the present.' The A.V. has 'now,' 'already,' 'now' ; the Vulgate *nunc, jam, nunc.* Again, 'the mystery of lawlessness' (τῆς ἀνομίας) has the closest connexion with 'the lawless one' (ὁ ἄνομος) in *v.* 8, the same power or person being meant. The A.V. has 'the mystery of iniquity' and 'that wicked,' where 'that' is another example of exaggeration in rendering the Greek article : see on '*this* calling' (i. 11) and '*that* man' (ii. 3). The Vulgate here has *ille iniquus* ; more often it has *hic* to represent the Greek article ; 1 Cor. i. 20, iii. 19, iv. 13 ; 2 Cor. v. 1 ; etc. Cf. the unfortunate change from 'life' to 'soul' Mt. xvi. 25, 26 ; from 'children' to 'sons' Mt. xx. 20 ; from 'rule' to 'line' 2 Cor. x. 15, 16 ; etc., etc.

be taken out of the way] Literally, 'out of the midst' (ἐκ μεσοῦ), as in 1 Cor. v. 2 ; in Col. ii. 14 we have ἐκ τοῦ μέσου. *E medio* or *de medio* is similarly used ; Vulg. has *de medio* here. It is clear from this that τὸ κατέχον cannot be the will of God, for in that case ὁ κατέχων would be God Himself, who cannot be taken out of the way.

St. Paul does not say *how* the restrainer will be removed, and perhaps he had no conviction on the subject. But he is convinced that the removal will take place, and the way be left clear for the revelation of the great mystery of evil. The context gives the impression that there will not be much delay. It is probably this utterance, that the restraining power will certainly be taken out of the way, and perhaps very soon, which caused him to use a cryptic description rather than a simple name. This the representatives of the power would understand and resent, and they would perhaps visit their resentment on both teachers and taught.* As Augustine says (*De Civ. Dei*, XX. xix. 2), these words "show that he was unwilling to speak openly, because he said that the Thessalonians knew. And therefore we, who do not know what the Thessalonians knew, would be glad even at the cost of much labour to arrive at the Apostle's meaning, but we cannot do it; all the less so, because what he goes on to say makes his meaning still more obscure. I frankly confess that I do not know what he means."

It is probable that much of the obscurity which besets our knowledge of the first ages of the Church is the result of Christians being unwilling to risk committing things plainly to writing. Silence and symbols were common devices.

There is, however, far less difficulty about the meaning of 'that which restraineth' and 'he that restraineth' than about the meaning of 'the Man of Lawlessness' and 'the Mystery of Lawlessness.' The change from the neuter to the masculine, from τὸ κατέχον to ὁ κατέχων, suggests the direction in which to look for an explanation. It suggests a power or principle of wide influence, which can either be readily personified, or be represented by some individual who possesses or symbolizes some of the leading characteristics. We have this at once in the Roman Empire and the Roman Emperor. This explanation fits the two expressions and their context so well, that it is almost a waste of time to look for any other; all the more so, because the large majority of commentators and critics, from Tertullian down to our own day, have accepted this interpretation as the right one. Tertullian, *Apol.* 32, says, "There is also another great necessity for us to pray for the Emperors, even for the whole state of the Empire and the fortunes of Rome, seeing that we know that the mighty force which

* We may compare the reticence of Josephus (*Ant.*, X. x. 4) about the interpretation of the 'stone' which was to destroy the Roman Empire, in Dan. ii. 35, 46; he can explain the past, but he does not venture to pry into the future. People must study Daniel for themselves, he says.

is menacing the whole world is being delayed by the respite allowed to the Roman Empire." See also *De Res. Carn.*, 24. Chrysostom and Jerome both suggest that St. Paul uses this circumlocution because the declaration that the Empire was to be abolished might provoke Roman magistrates to persecute. Harnack says that by τὸ κατέχον we must understand the Roman Empire, which, so far from being the opponent of the Church, was at that time keeping in check the terrible evils which threatened it (*The Expansion of Christianity*, I. p. 258). The natural restrainer of lawlessness is the law, and in the first century the great organizer and executor of the law was the Roman Empire. Christ Himself had taught this; 'Whose is this image and superscription?' Mk. xii. 16, 17; Mt. xxii. 21, 22; Lk. xx. 24, 25. St. Paul had followed Him; Rom. xiii. 1–7. Both he and Silvanus were Roman citizens, a condition which they knew to be both an honour and a protection. At Thessalonica the politarchs had paid little attention to the unsupported accusations of the fanatical Jews, and had let the accused go free (Acts xvii. 8); and at Corinth, where this letter was written, Gallio, the Roman proconsul, protected the Apostle from the attacks of his Jewish persecutors in that city. It was precisely this Roman power, the merits of which Christ and St. Paul upheld, that the Jews were feverishly eager to overthrow; and they would regard no one as the Messiah who could not or would not overthrow it. The probabilities are altogether in favour of the theory that the restraining power which St. Paul has here in his mind is the Roman Empire as the great upholder of human law in its best forms. History has shown us that although each Roman ruler was destined to fall, and the Roman Empire itself to be overrun by barbaric conquerors, yet Roman Law has survived all shocks. It has joined with the Gospel in producing large departments of Christian legislation designed for the restraining of evil. See Renan, *Hibbert Lectures*, pp. 185 f., for St. Luke's view.

Those who reject this interpretation of the power that restrains suggest, among other conjectures, the Holy Spirit, or a powerful angel, or Elijah (Mt. xvii. 11), or St. Paul himself, or the prayers of Christians, or Satan as 'the god of this age' (2 Cor. iv. 4). We need not discuss any of them. Nor is there any need, with regard to 'he who for the present is restraining,' to fix on any particular Emperor; and it is difficult to think of such rulers as Caligula and Nero in the character of checks upon evil-doing. But we know that St. Paul could regard the position which they held, and the system which they maintained, as 'a terror to the evil work' and 'an avenger for wrath to him that doeth evil' (Rom. xiii. 3, 4). See Frame *ad loc.* for a summary of views.

8–12. *The Terrible End of the Lawless One.*

8 And then shall that wicked be revealed, whom the Lord shall consume with the spirit of his mouth, and shall destroy with the brightness of his coming: 9 *Even him* whose coming is after the working of Satan, with all power and signs, and lying wonders, 10 And with all deceivableness of unrighteousness, in them that perish: because they received not the love of the truth, that they might be saved. 11 And for this cause God shall send them strong delusion, that they should believe a lie: 12 That they all might be damned who believed not the truth, but had pleasure in unrighteousness.

The Apostle passes from the present condition of things (*vv.* 6, 7) which he does not care to describe in detail, because the Thessalonians know it from their own experience, and passes on to the future, with regard to which they had been seriously misled.

8 And then, and not till then, the Lawless One will be revealed, whose dominion will be brief, for the Lord Jesus will slay him with the breath of His mouth, and will bring him to nought by the very manifestation of His own Presence at His Coming, the Lord's Presence utterly bringing to nought that of him 9 whose Presence at his coming is in full accordance with the working of Satan. For he will imitate the Lord with every kind of supernatural power, and of miraculous signs, and of bewildering wonders, for the purpose of deluding men. 10 And he will work with every kind of wicked device for the deceiving of those who are already on the road to perdition, seeing that they refused to welcome the love of truth which was offered to them with a view to their salvation. 11 So, because of this fatal refusal, *God* sends them (this is their certain doom) an inward

predilection for error, leading them to choose to believe what is false ; 12 and He does this to bring a judgment on *all* those who refused to believe the truth, but on the contrary took pleasure in unrighteousness.

8. **And then**] When the restraining power has been removed. 'Then' is in contrast to the preceding 'now,' 'already,' 'for the present'; cf. 1 Cor. iv. 5; Mk. xiii. 26, 27. As already pointed out, the A.V. obliterates the obvious connexion between 'the mystery of lawlessness' (τὸ μυστήριον τῆς ἀνομίας) and 'the lawless one' (ὁ ἄνομος). Both expressions indicate the consummate rebellion against all law and authority. The Apostle has a good deal more to say about its methods and success (9–12), but he lessens the horror of this announcement by first foretelling its utter failure and destruction. Cf. *Assumption of Moses*, X. 7–9; *Apocalypse of Baruch*, XL. 1–3.

the Lord Jesus] The A.V. follows some good authorities in omitting 'Jesus'; but the balance is in favour of retaining it. It is absent of course from Is. xi. 4, which St. Paul is here adapting with a change of wording; and this may have led to its omission here.

slay him] The A.V. has 'consume,' the translation of a reading (ἀναλώσει) which is probably false. The R.V. has 'slay' (ἀνελεῖ), which has far greater authority; see Plummer on Lk. xxii. 2. But both readings may be variants from a third (ἀναλοῖ). Something depends upon the interpretation of 'with the breath of His mouth';—'breath' (R.V.) rather 'spirit' (A.V.). In Is. xi. 'with the breath of His lips' seems to mean that a single utterance will suffice to slay the wicked. So Theodore, Chrysostom, and Theodoret understand it, while Athanasius seems to have understood it of the Holy Spirit. The phrase is said to have been a current Jewish periphrasis. Thus Ps. xxxii. (xxxiii.) 6 the stars are said to be made τῷ πνεύματι τοῦ στόματος αὐτοῦ: Enoch lxii. 2 "the word of his mouth (the Messiah's) slew all the sinners": Ps. of Solomon xvii. 27, "He shall destroy the ungodly nations with the word of his mouth" (again of the Messiah). But St. Paul seems to mean that the Lord's breath is to be an instrument of destruction, sweeping away like a hurricane, or killing like the blast from a furnace. If 'with a word' is the meaning, 'consume' is not very suitable; but 'slay' agrees with either interpretation. Swete on Rev. ii. 16 remarks that "the glorified Christ is in this book a warrior, who fights with the sharp sword of the word"; cf. xix. 13; Eph. vi. 17; Heb. iv. 12. Charles on Rev. i. 16, "The sword that proceeds from the mouth of the Son of Man is simply a symbol of his judicial authority," Cf. 4 Ezra xiii. 10, 38.

bring him to nought] Literally, 'render him inoperative,' 'put him out of action' (καταργέω). The verb is eminently Pauline. It occurs 27 times in N.T., and 25 of these are in the writings of St. Paul, especially in the four great Epistles. The A.V. is marvellously capricious. No single English word would suffice; but we do not need 15 or more different renderings; 'cumber,' 'make without effect,' 'make void,' 'make of none effect,' 'destroy,' 'loose,' 'bring to nought,' 'do away,' 'put away,' put down,' and (for the passive) 'come to nought,' 'fail,' 'vanish away,' 'abolished,' 'fallen away.' We need a strong word here; 'disarm' is almost a bathos after 'destroy.' See Schürer, *The Jewish People in the Time of Jesus Christ,* Div. II., vol. ii., pp. 164 ff. on the last attack, and the destruction, of the hostile powers.

by the very manifestation of His own Presence] Literally, 'by the Epiphany of His Presence,' or 'His Coming' (τῇ ἐπιφανείᾳ τῆς παρουσίας αὐτοῦ); see on *v.* 1 for παρουσία. 'Epiphany' in LXX is often used of manifestations of the glory of God. This use is specially common in 2 Maccabees. In pagan inscriptions it is usual of the apparition of a god. But, as Clemen remarks (*Primitive Christianity,* pp. 341, 371), if we have here "a pagan mode of speech, it is only the *expression* that is borrowed, not the idea." For the combination of ἐπιφανεία with παρουσία see Deissmann, *Light from the Ancient East,* pp. 374, 378. Alford, followed by Bishop Alexander, quotes Milton's "Far off His Coming shone" (*Par. Lost,* vi. 768).

Excepting the present passage, the word is found in N.T.

in the Pastoral Epistles only, and there it occurs five times. In 2 Tim. i. 10 it is used of the First Advent of Christ, and there we also have καταργέω of the abolition of death. In the other passages it is used, as here, of the Second Advent; 1 Tim. vi. 14; 2 Tim. iv. 1, 8; Titus ii. 13. Here the A.V. has 'brightness.' Vulg. has *illustratio* here, and *illuminatio* 2 Tim. i. 10. Other renderings are *apparentia* and *apparitio*. The meaning possibly may be that, just as the 'light from heaven above the brightness of the sun' (Acts xxvi. 13) reduced to impotence Saul the persecutor of the Lord, so the brightness of the Second Advent will reduce to impotence the great adversary of Christ. St. Paul's own experience may have suggested the idea of the Lawless One being sent to nothingness by the glory of the manifestation. *Christum suis radiis, quos ante adventum suum emittet, tenebras Antichristi profligaturum* (Calvin).

9. **Whose Presence is**] We might have had ἀποκάλυψις here in harmony with ἀποκαλύπτεσθαι above (*vv.* 3, 6, 8); yet we have παρουσία, less for the sake of variety than to emphasize the parallel with Christ. Note 'is' (ἐστιν) of what is the essential character.

in full accordance with the activity of Satan] This is conclusive against the view that the great adversary is Satan, a view which is found in the *Apostolical Constitutions*, vii. 32. He has diabolical malignity and power; he is Satan's ally and supreme agent; but he is not the evil one himself. That St. Paul believed in Satan as a personal agent of evil is beyond a doubt; and 'Satan' is always a proper name; 1 Thess. ii. 18; Rom. xvi. 20; 1 Cor. v. 5, vii. 5; 2 Cor. ii. 11, xi. 14; 1 Tim. i. 20, v. 15. Elsewhere he calls him 'the tempter,' 1 Thess. iii. 5; 'the serpent,' 2 Cor. xi. 3; 'the god of this age,' 2 Cor. iv. 4; 'the devil,' Eph. iv. 27, etc.; 'the evil one,' Eph. vi. 16.

'Activity' or 'working' (ἐνέργεια) is a neutral word and may be used of the worst, as well as of the best, of operations. Excepting here and *v.* 11, it is always used in N.T. of the Divine activity; Eph. i. 19, iii. 7, iv. 16; Phil. iii. 21; Col. i. 29, ii. 12;—all instances being in the Epistles of St. Paul, and in all, excepting Col. ii. 12, we have κατὰ τὴν ἐνέργειαν or κατ' ἐνέργειαν, as here. On the use of κατά in such expressions, which are very frequent in Paul, see Westcott, *Ephesians*, pp. 12, 30, 195. 'After' (A.V.) is ambiguous, and might be misunderstood; 'according to' (R.V.) is better. That an expression commonly used of Divine activity is here used of what is Satanic is probably not accidental; it is part of the parallel which throughout this passage is drawn between Divine and diabolical operations.

with every kind of power . . . signs . . . wonders] This threefold description of what we call 'miracles' is found Acts ii. 22; Rom. xv. 19; 2 Cor. xii. 12; Heb. ii. 4; but 'power' is often plural, 'mighty works' (δυνάμεις), and is used in Mt. and Mk. of the miracles wrought by Christ. St. John calls them 'signs' (σημεῖα), a word which he uses 17 times; he never calls them 'powers.' Miracles are signs of Christ's Divine mission, and are symbolical of spiritual truths. Nowhere in the N.T. are they called simply 'wonders' (τέρατα); they are not regarded as mere prodigies to excite astonishment. Wherever 'wonders' is used it is always combined, as here, with 'signs,' and the usual combination is 'signs and wonders,' not 'wonders and signs.' 'Signs' is the word most frequently found in Scripture, with or without another synonymous term. It is hardly necessary to point out that miracles imply power, and experience teaches that they excite wonder. It is because wonder is so obvious that 'miracle' has become the current term. It has the disadvantage of expressing what is only a secondary characteristic, but the advantage of committing us to nothing but what is certainly true. For signs wrought by evil powers to deceive mankind see Rev. xiii. 13, 14, xvi. 14, xix. 20. See Charles on Rev. xiii. 13.

Although 'all' or 'every kind of' (πάσῃ) agrees in gender with 'power' (δυνάμει) only, yet it is undoubtedly to be carried on to both 'signs' and 'wonders.' Similarly, the characterizing genitive (ψεύδους), 'for the purpose of deluding,' does not belong to 'wonders' only, as A.V. and R.V.

might lead us to suppose, but looks back to 'signs' and 'power' also. All three are 'lying,' not in the sense that they are shams, but that they are wrought to induce people to believe what is false. Theodore and Theodoret and Jerome seem to understand that they were sham miracles. Chrysostom and Augustine (*De Civ. Dei*, xx. 19) leave the question open. But these signs and wonders are real miracles.; they cannot be explained by any known laws; and they are manifested 'that they may lead astray, if possible, the elect' (Mk. xiii. 22; Mt. xxiv. 24). *L'epouvante devint ainsi un élément de toute apocalypse; il fut admis que le mal, près de finir, allait redoubler de rage et faire preuve d'un art savant pour exterminer les saints* (Renan, *L'Antechrist*, p. 330). Consummate deceit, making evil look like good, is of the very nature of the devil; Jn. viii. 44; Rev. xii. 9, xx. 3, 8, 10; cf. xiii. 13, 14.

10. **with every kind of wicked device**] The same construction as before (ἐν πάσῃ ἀπάτῃ ἀδικίας); 'of wickedness' or 'of unrighteousness' being a characterizing genitive equivalent to an adjective, as in 'man of lawlessness' *v.* 3. 'Deceivableness' (A.V.) is quite wrong: 'deceit' (Eph. iv. 22; Col. ii. 8) or 'deceitfulness' (Heb. iii. 13) is the meaning. But these terrific powers are not irresistible; only those who are already predisposed fall victims. "Paul is quite content with a general description of the circumstances attending the advent of the *Anomos*; but later descriptions of the Antichrist delight in the details, *e.g.* Rev. xiii. 13; Asc. Isa. v. 4; Sib. Orac. iii. 63, ii. 167; see Bousset, *Antichrist*, 115 ff., and Charles on Asc. Isa. v. 4" (Frame, *Thessalonians*, p. 269).

are already on the road to perdition] the present participle τοῖς ἀπολλυμένοις) implies that perishing has already begun, not that perdition has already taken place. Nevertheless, the classification is made in accordance with their present position: and, although there is no idea of *predestination* to perdition, yet that end is regarded for the moment as certain. It is important in translation to preserve the connexion between 'son of perdition' (ἀπωλείας) and 'those who are on the way to perdition' (οἱ ἀπολλύμενοι). Abbott, *Son of Man*, p. 350. We must also carefully compare 1 Cor. i. 18 and 2 Cor. ii. 15, where 'those who are perishing' are the antithesis to 'those who are being saved' or 'are on the road to salvation' (οἱ σωζόμενοι); cf. Lk. xiii. 23; Acts ii. 47. The two classes indicate the issues of faith and of unbelief, of obedience and of rebellion. St. Paul nowhere defines 'perishing,' and it is rash for us to do so as meaning 'annihilation,' or 'endless torment.' He calls the end of unbelievers 'death' (Rom. vi. 23, viii. 6), 'corruption' (Gal. vi. 8), and 'wrath' (1 Thess. i. 10, v. 9). But he has much less to say about this class than about those who by believing can secure salvation. Those will be seduced who deserve to be seduced (Augustine) and who would have remained in disobedience, if the great adversary had not appeared (Chrysostom). See Leo the Great, *Ep.* 129, on the way in which statements made for salvation may, by a subtle change, be turned to destruction.

seeing that] Or, 'for the reason that,' 'because' (ἀνθ' ὧν); frequent in LXX, but elsewhere in N.T. in Lk. and Acts only. We might say 'in requital for their refusal.'

to welcome] Cf. 1 Thess. i. 6, ii. 13, where the same verb (δέχομαι) is used of receiving with joy, accepting willingly. This meaning is frequent; 1 Cor. ii. 14; 2 Cor. viii. 17; Gal. iv. 14; Col. iv. 10; etc.

the love of the truth] Mere rejection of the truth might be the result of blindness or ignorance; but these sinners would not cultivate any *affection* for the truth and did not desire to obtain it. They were already grievously astray; and so 'they loved the darkness rather than the light' (Jn. iii. 19). Here, as in 1 Cor. xiii. 6 and 2 Cor. xiii. 8, 'the truth' is used in its widest sense; truth as opposed to unrighteousness (Rom. ii. 8), and therefore as equivalent to goodness; cf. Jn. iii. 21; 1 Jn. i. 6. In Ps. l. (li.) 8 and lxxxiii. (lxxxiv.) 12 God is said ἀλήθειαν ἀγαπᾶν.

with a view to] The same construction is in *v.* 6 and 1 Thess. ii. 12.

their salvation] The opposite of the perdition which is the end of their present course. It includes deliverance from sin in this world and from condemnation in the next. It is offered to all men; but they are left free to accept it or reject it.

11. **So because of this**] *Καί* is here consecutive, introducing a result of what has just been stated; we use 'so' in a similar way. 'Because of this' looks back to 'seeing that' (ἀνθ' ὧν) in *v.* 10.

God sends them] 'God' is emphatic; even Satanic power works under His control. God establishes laws which have their natural course. The eye that lives in the dark becomes blind; the limb that is never moved loses the power of movement; in morals, the will that never chooses good loses the power to choose it, and thus sin is punished by sin.

The present tense is often used of what is predicted with confidence. Some copyists, not understanding the predictive present, changed πέμπει to πέμψει, and this reading of some inferior authorities is followed in A.V., '*shall* send.' Theodoret, Jerome, and Augustine water this down to meaning that God will *allow* this to happen.

an inward predilection for error] This seems to be the meaning of 'a working of error' (ἐνέργειαν πλάνης). After allowing themselves to be led astray through their indifference to truth, they become active propagators of what is grievously wrong. 'Strong delusion' (A.V.) is misleading; it comes from Tyndale through the Genevan Version. The Vulgate has *operatio erroris*, Beza *Efficacia deceptionis*. Cf. Is. lxiii. 17, and διὰ τοῦτο ἐκέρασεν αὐτοῖς ὁ Θεὸς πνεῦμα πλανήσεως Ps. of Solomon viii. 15. There are these stages in their downward course. They refuse to receive the truth. They have no wish to attain to it, but prefer unrighteousness. God sends them as a punishment a predilection for error.

believe what is false] Not merely 'a lie,' but 'the lie' (τὸ ψεῦδος), the opposite of 'the truth' (*v.* 10), and therefore that which is morally evil. Persistent defiance of conscience deprives it of discernment and power. Do what you know to be wrong once or twice, and you will then think that it is not so very wrong. Do it many times, and you will cease to think that it is wrong at all. This may often be observed with regard to untruthfulness and dishonesty; but it holds good in other forms of sin also.

12. **to bring a judgment**] That the judgment will be a condemnation is shown by the context, but this does not justify such a translation as 'be damned.' The Greek verb (κρίνω) is neutral and may be used of a favourable judgment; Acts iii. 13, xv. 19, xvi. 15, xxi. 25. Even the compound, which implies condemnation (κατακρίνω), does not justify 'damn,' which is now commonly understood as meaning condemning to hell, although in the seventeenth and earlier centuries it was by no means restricted to this meaning. See the A.V. of [Mk.] xvi. 16 and Rom. xiv. 23. Similarly, κρίμα, 'judgment,' is rendered 'damnation,' Rom. xiii. 2 and 1 Cor. xi. 29. This unfortunate translation has cost the Anglican Church multitudes of communicants, for the exhortation in the Prayer Book contains the Apostle's warning against communicating unworthily in this disastrously repellent form. People doubt whether they are worthy, and, in fear of condemning themselves to hell, abstain from communicating. Lightfoot, *On a Fresh Revision*, p. 72; Wright, *Bible Word-Book*, p. 181; Davies, *Bible English*, p. 96. Here Rutherford and Moffatt have 'be doomed.'

on all those] The 'all' comes after the verb with emphasis and perhaps we ought to read the strong form ἅπαντες, 'all of them together,' 'every one of them,' rather than the simple πάντες, 'all.' The diabolical campaign has been grievously successful, and the evil is widespread. *Late et diu et vehementer grassatur error ille* (Bengel). The point that is certain, and on which the Apostle lays stress, is this. A judgment of condemnation is among the purposes of God; and not one of those who have incurred it by their deliberate conduct will escape. What form the condemnation will take he does not attempt to define.

refused to believe the truth] This looks back to *v.* 10. They rejected what they recognized, or might readily have recognized, as morally good. And that was not the whole of their revolt; 'on the contrary' (ἀλλά).

took pleasure in unrighteousness] This also looks back to *v.* 10, where we are told that it was a 'device of unrighteousness,' a wicked and deceitful plan, to which they surrendered themselves. They not only had no love for what was right, they had good-will towards the very opposite. Chrysostom takes 'unrighteousness' to mean the Antichrist.

Now, with such details—sufficient for the Thessalonians—as the Apostle gives before us, we are in a better position to examine the question whether he describes a person or a principle of evil. We have seen that '*that* which restraineth' (τὸ κατέχον) is almost certainly the Roman Empire, which may be personified as '*he* who restraineth' (ὁ κατέχων), any Emperor being regarded as a representative of the organization. It is therefore possible that 'the Man of Lawlessness, may be a personification also, a personification of the 'many Antichrists' which were at work when St. John wrote his Epistle, 1 Jn. ii. 8. St. Paul in like manner says that 'the mystery of lawlessness' is already working, although the moving cause has not yet been revealed.

But the two cases are not quite parallel. In the case of the restraint on lawlessness the impersonal expression, '*that* which restraineth,' is used first, as if this was the proper designation, and the personal form is not repeated. In the case of the evil power which for the present is held in check the personal expression comes first, and it is repeated again and again; 'the man of lawlessness,' 'the son of perdition,' 'he that opposeth and exalteth himself,' 'setting him forth as God,' 'the lawless one whom,' etc. Only once have we an impersonal expression, 'the mystery of lawlessness.'

Nor is this all. From first to last this appalling being is represented as a parallel, or parody,—one might almost say an impious caricature, of the position and work of Christ. The Apostle seems to have felt "a kind of necessity that Christ and Antichrist should alternate with one another," the latter being a *sorte de messie de Satan . . . L'inverse exact de Jésus, comme une sorte de Christ de L'enfer* (Renan,

Saint Paul, p. 253). As Christ is the emissary and agent and representative of God, so this monstrous being is the emissary and agent and representative of Satan. The Coming of both was matter of prophecy, for the Apostle's description is partly inspired by visions in Daniel. Both have a revelation, and both have an influence in the world before the revelation takes place. Just as the First Coming of Christ caused a crisis, a separation of the lovers of light from the lovers of darkness (Jn. iii. 10), so this Coming of the great adversary separates those who love the truth from those who take pleasure in unrighteousness. As Christ does mighty works and signs and wonders for the instruction and salvation of mankind, so also does he for their deception and ruin. As Christ came to seek and to save those who were lost, so this rival comes to complete the perdition of those who are perishing. Christ proclaimed Himself to be the Son of God and one with the Father ; this opponent exalts himself above everything that is worshipped, and proclaims to the world that he himself is God. " It must have been a great, deeply religious spirit who created this conception, one proof more of the genuine Pauline origin of our Epistle." (Dobschütz, p. 296, quoted by Frame.) See Charles on Rev. xiii. 13 ; Ramsay, *Letters to the Seven Churches*, pp. 101 f.

All this seems to point to an individual, of superhuman power and craftiness, and with a supremely evil will ; and we cannot wonder that such was the almost universal belief of the early Church. It was held that, before the Second Advent, a false Christ would establish on earth a reign of extraordinary wickedness, which, however, would soon be ended by the Return of the true Christ in glory.

It does not, of course, follow from this that the theory of a personal Antichrist is the right theory. That the whole is a picturesque personification of the manifold powers of evil is an explanation which may seem to be improbable, but which cannot be disproved. " St. Paul may have seen in some actual adversary of the Gospel a type of the antichristian spirit and working ; and this may have facilitated the personification " (Lightfoot). Jowett regards the Man of Sin as " the impersonation of sin . . . the image of self-destroying evil. . . . There is no reason to suppose that the description refers to an individual. . . . As Christ is a person, so evil is impersonated as his antagonist." *En face de Jésus, se dresse un monstre qui est l'idéal du mal, de même que Jésus est l'idéal du bien* (Renan, *L'Antechrist*, p. ii.).

A summary and estimate of Chrysostom's treatment of the whole passage (3–12) is given by Chase, *Chrysostom, a Study in Biblical Interpretation*, pp. 168 f. Cyril of Jerusalem (*Catech.*, xv. 11) makes the enemy a false Messiah (Mt. xxiv. 24): " shall falsely style himself Christ." Theodoret, " calling himself Christ and God." Jerome, " showing himself off as if he himself were Christ and the Son of God." We may conclude with the words of Augustine; *Melius est dubitare de rebus occultis, quam litigare de incertis.*

ii. 13–15. Thanksgiving and Exhortation

13 But we are bound to give thanks alway to God for you, brethren,
beloved of the Lord, because God hath from the beginning chosen
you to salvation, through sanctification of the spirit, and belief of
the truth, 14 Whereunto he called you by our Gospel, to the obtaining
of the glory of the Lord Jesus Christ. 15 Therefore, brethren, stand
fast, and hold the traditions which ye have been taught, whether
by word or our Epistle.

The writers have said enough about this sorrowful prospect of the ruin of many. They gladly turn away from it, to give thanks to God that their beloved Thessalonians are among the elect who are in the way of salvation, and to exhort them to secure this blessed result by following the instructions given to them. These faithful converts form a refreshing contrast to the unhappy victims of the Antichrist; and those who converted them are bound to give thanks for them, and to endeavour to help them onwards in the good way which by God's grace they have chosen.

This contrast should be compared with that in 1 Thess. ii. 12–iii. 13, which is similar in arrangement, and also v.

2–8, where the mention of the Day of the Lord suggests the difference which it will make between the sons of light and the sons of darkness, and leads on to an exhortation to be sober and spiritually minded. But the exhortation in *v.* 15 has no parallel in the First Epistle.

13 But *we*, when we think of this terrible result of persisting in wickedness, continually feel bound, and cannot help feeling bound, to give thanks to the one and only God on all occasions for you, Brethren, who have been and are so dearly beloved, not only by us but by the Lord Jesus, because God chose you from all eternity to have the offer of salvation, an offer which has become effectual through the sanctifying influence of His Holy Spirit and your acceptance and retention of the truth. 14 It was to this state of salvation that He called you by means of the Gospel of good tidings which we preach to the world, with a view to the securing by you of glory, viz., a share in the glory of our Lord Jesus Christ. 15 Seeing therefore, Brethren, that such is God's gracious purpose respecting you, and such your realization of it, you must of course continue to stand stedfast and firm, and to hold fast and fully all the heaven-sent instruction in faith and conduct that we handed on to you, whether by word of mouth while we were with you, or by letter since we left.

13. **But we**] 'But' marks the contrast between the writers' horror of what has just been described and their thankfulness for their converts' escape from such ruin. The emphatic 'we' (ἡμεῖς δὲ ὀφείλομεν), which is absent in i. 3, links the happiness of the writers with that of their converts. They might quite naturally have said 'But *you*,' in contrast with 'those who are perishing.'

continually feel bound] See notes on i. 3. Here ὀφείλομεν comes first with much emphasis, and hence the repetition of 'feel bound' in the paraphrase.

beloved by the Lord] In 1 Thess. i. 4 we have, at a similar point in the Thanksgiving, 'beloved by God,' a unique expression in the N.T. In Deut. xxxiii. 12 Benjamin is called 'beloved by the Lord,' which of course means by Jehovah. In Ecclus. xlv. 1 Moses is said to be 'beloved by God and men.' In the Testaments, *Issachar* i. 1, we have 'beloved by the Lord' applied to either Issachar, or his sons, or his words (readings vary). The change here from 'beloved by God' to 'beloved by the Lord' is remarkable, because, according to Pauline usage (see on 1 Thess. i. 6, iii. 12, iv. 15, 16, v. 2), 'the Lord' means 'the Lord Jesus Christ,' and the two expressions seem to be treated as equivalent. That 'the Lord' here means Christ is the more certain because 'God' precedes and follows; the change of word suggests a change of Person. The perfect participle (ἠγαπημένοι) implies present result of past action (Burton, *N.T. Moods and Tenses*, § 154); hence 'have been and are so dearly beloved.' This affectionate and impressive address is calculated to calm and recover the excited and disorderly members.

chose you] The verb (εἵλατο) is rare in Bibl. Grk., and is not used elsewhere in N.T. of election (ἐκλέγεσθαι) by God. In Deut. xxvi. 18 it occurs of God's choosing Israel as a peculiar people. Deut. vii. 6, 7, x. 15 we have προείλατο. There is no emphasis on you, and therefore no special contrast with 'those who are perishing.' The reading 'us' may safely be rejected. Confusion between ὑμεῖς and ἡμεῖς in MSS. is very common; 2 Cor. i. 11, iii. 2, v. 12, vi. 16, vii. 12 (*bis*), etc.

from all eternity] The reading is uncertain. This rendering follows that which has the better authority, ἀπ' ἀρχῆς. If it is right, there is little doubt that 'from the beginning' means from 'from all eternity,' equivalent to 'before the foundation of the world' (Eph. i. 4; 1 Pet. i. 20; Jn. xvii. 24) and 'before the ages' (1 Cor. ii. 7). See Hort. on 1 Pet. i. 20 and Westcott on Eph. i. 4. But 'as the firstfruits,' ἀπαρχήν (R.V. marg.), has strong support, makes good sense, and is more in harmony with St. Paul's style; 1 Cor. xv. 20, 23, xvi. 15; also Rom. viii. 23, xi. 16, and xvi. 5, where the readings vary as they do here. The Philippians and the Thessalonians were converted during the same mission, and were firstfruits of the West; 1 Thess. i. 7.

If 'chose you from all eternity' is right, it does not imply predestination to final salvation. The Apostle warns them that they may lose what God has willed to offer them. They must secure it, not merely by closing with His offer, as they did when they accepted the Gospel, but also by being stedfast in belief and conduct, in accordance with teaching already received. They are not predestined to glory, but invited to win it for themselves by a holy life; Phil. ii. 12.

to have the offer of salvation] God placed them in the way of being saved when the missionaries preached to them and He gave them grace to listen. The final confirmation of His gracious purpose comes at the Last Day. "Paul lets his religious imagination range from everlasting to everlasting,—from the choice of God before the foundation of the world to the consummation in the age to come. . . . The purpose of this pregnant summary of Paul's religious convictions (cf. Rom. viii. 28–30) is the encouragement of the faint-hearted" (Frame, p. 279).

through the sanctifying influence of the Holy Spirit] The phrase (*ἐν ἁγιασμῷ πνεύματος*) is ambiguous. We have the same words 1 Pet. i. 2, which is probably based on this passage. There the order of the words, 'God the Father, Spirit, Jesus Christ' is decisive for Holy Spirit rather than human spirit. Here the order points in the same direction; first the Divine influence, then the faith of the persons influenced. In both passages 'Holy' is omitted as superfluous after 'sanctification' (*ἁγίου* after *ἁγιασμῷ*). The absence of the article before 'Spirit' proves nothing. There are several passages in the Epistles, especially in the phrase *ἐν πνεύματι*, in which we are in doubt whether the Holy Spirit or man's spirit is meant. "The believer is separated by so thin a film from the Spirit of God that the operation of the one is often in Scripture transferred to the other, and language wavers in meaning between the two or seems to comprehend both" (Jowett on i. 11). See Hort on 1 Pet. i. 2 and Westcott on Eph. iii. 6. With most commentators we may decide for the higher meaning here. Thus we have all three Persons of the Trinity; Thanks to the Father for those who are beloved by the Son and sanctified by the Spirit. From this passage, combined with Mt. xxviii. 19; 2 Cor. xiii. 14; 1 Pet. i. 1, 2; Jude 20, 21, it is evident that "the naming of the Father, the Lord Jesus, and the Spirit together must have been frequent" (Clemen, *Primitive Christianity*, p. 204). See Plummer, *S. Matthew*, pp. 431 f., and *2 Corinthians*, p. 384. The term ἁγιασμός implies a *process* of sanctification, and in N.T. it is chiefly Pauline; 1 Thess. iv. 3, 7; Rom. vi. 19, 22; 1 Cor. i. 30; 1 Tim. ii. 15. This is the Divine side; the human side follows, and we see from their combination under one preposition (ἐν, Winer, p. 519) that growth in sanctification and true knowledge is regarded as simultaneous (Chadwick, *Pastoral Teaching of St. Paul*, pp. 157 f.). See Charles on Rev. vii. 3, pp. 196, 205, 206.

your acceptance and retention of the truth] This is implied in ἐν πίστει ἀληθείας, which looks back to 'those who refused to believe the truth' (*v.* 12). The writers are deeply thankful that the Thessalonians were among those who readily accepted it and have retained it. Cf. the joy expressed in Col. ii. 5.

The genitives in this verse illustrate Deissmann's remark (*St. Paul*, pp. 140 f.) that the Apostle's use of the genitive is sometimes very peculiar and transcends all rules about subjective and objective. He suggests "mystic genitive" for him. A. T. Robertson, *Gr. of Grk. N.T.*, p. 501. Cf. ii. 11.

14. **to this state of salvation**] The neuter pronoun (εἰς ὅ) shows that the whole of the previous statement is to be understood.

He called you] God is the great Inviter (ὁ καλῶν, 1 Thess. ii. 12, v. 24). Here we have the aorist (ἐκάλεσεν) in harmony with 'chose' (εἵλατο) in *v.* 13. The choice was made from all eternity; the invitation to realize it was given when the missionaries began to preach at Thessalonica. Cf. 1 Thess. iv. 7; Rom. viii. 30. This use of καλεῖν is thoroughly Pauline; it occurs in all four groups, and especially in Romans, 1 Corinthians, Galatians, and Ephesians. We may safely retain the reading ὑμᾶς, although ἡμᾶς has considerable support.

which we preach to the world] Literally, '*our* Gospel' (τὸ εὐαγγέλιον ἡμῶν): cf. 1 Thess. i. 5, ii. 9. 'Our' refers to the senders of the letter, Paul, Silvanus, and Timothy, just as in 2 Cor. iv. 3 'our' refers to Paul and Timothy. In Rom. ii. 16, xvi. 25 and 2 Tim. ii. 8 we have 'my Gospel,' 'that which I preach,' for in sending those two letters the Apostle names no colleague. See on i. 3 and 1 Thess. i. 2, ii. 13. Neither here nor there is there any reference to a written Gospel. St. Paul may possibly have known 'Q,' the document used by both Mt. and Lk., but it is not likely that even the earliest of our four Gospels was in existence when St. Paul wrote. Irenaeus (III. ii. 8) is apparently the earliest writer who uses εὐαγγέλιον of a written Gospel. See McGiffert on Eus. *H.E.* III. iv. 8.

with a view to the securing] We have the same phrase, εἰς περιποίησιν 1 Thess. v. 9 and Heb. x. 39, and the meaning is the same in all three places,—*in acquisitionem* (Vulg.).

glory of our Lord Jesus Christ] That which He possesses as Lord and which He will exhibit in the Day of the Lord. It is an entrancing element in the salvation then won. This eschatological sense of 'glory,' as denoting the final state of the redeemed, is characteristic of St. Paul (1 Cor. ii. 7, xv. 43; Rom. v. 2; Phil. iii. 21; 1 Thess. ii. 12; etc.) and, excepting Heb. ii. 10 and 1 Pet. v. 1, 10, is almost peculiar to him. Cf. 2 Tim. ii. 10. 'Glory' is a contrast to 'wrath,' as 'salvation' to 'perdition': all four are eschatological terms. Kennedy, *St. Paul's Conception of the Last Things*, pp. 299 f.

15. **Seeing therefore**] The connecting particles (Ἄρα οὖν) introduce the practical conclusion of what has just been stated respecting the blessed condition of the Thessalonian converts; they must strive earnestly not to fall from it by misconduct. God's gracious election and calling do not act magically or irresistibly; those who receive must co-operate; Heb. iii. 14; 2 Pet. i. 10.

continue to stand stedfast and firm] Present imperative of the strong form στήκω, which is frequent in St. Paul, especially in exhortations; 1 Cor. xvi. 13; Gal. v. 1; Phil. i. 27, iv. 1. See on 1 Thess. iii. 8. The fact that God has chosen and invited them must not lead to presumptuous slackness; it ought to constrain them to respond to it with a loyal stedfastness,—the very opposite of σαλευθῆναι (*v.* 2).

hold fast and fully all . . . that we handed on to you] The verb is very rare in the Epistles; only here and Col. ii. 19 with the accusative; Heb. iv. 14, vi. 18 with the genitive. With the acc. it means keeping firm hold of the whole which is possessed or is to be possessed, as here, κρατεῖτε τὰς παραδόσεις. Cf. Rev. ii. 13, 25, iii. 11. With the gen. it means laying hold of a part, attaching oneself to, when there is no full possession; *e.g.* τῆς χειρός Mk. v. 41, ix. 27; Mt. ix. 25; Lk. viii. 54. See Westcott on κρατῶμεν τῆς ὁμολογίας Heb. iv. 14. The acc. is much more common. Vulg. has *state et tenete*; Beza *perstate et retinete*, which is better. The Thessalians possessed the instructions handed on to them; they must take care to keep them in their entirety, *nil addentes, nil detrahentes. Traditio est ingens possessio* (Bengel). Κατέχειν is more often used in this sense than κρατεῖν; 1 Cor. xi. 2; 1 Thess. v. 21.

The Apostle habitually uses παραδόσεις and παραδιδόναι of his teaching, which is not his own invention. He received it directly or indirectly from God (1 Cor. xi. 2, 23, xv. 3), and he passes it on to others. Cf. παραγγέλλομεν iii. 4, 6, 10, 12. Conversely, his hearers are said παραλαμβάνειν what he passes on to them; iii. 6, 1 Thess. ii. 13, iv. 1; 1 Cor. xv. 1, 2; Phil. iv. 9.

whether by word of mouth . . . or by letter] The A.V. is misleading. 'Our' (ἡμῶν) belongs to both substantives, 'whether by our word or by our letter.' The converts are to regard letters from their instructors as of equal authority with their oral teaching. Lightfoot points out that this passage is fatal to the distinction which in later times gained currency, between the written word and oral tradition. "Tradition in the scriptural sense may be either written or oral."

With this appeal to tradition compare 1 Cor. xi. 23, xv. 3; Rom. vi. 17; 2 Tim. i. 13. In view of such passages as these, "it is gratuitous," as Moffatt remarks, to read any second-century passion for oral apostolic tradition into these words or into those of iii. 6.

16, 17. Prayer for the Thessalonians

The combination of thanksgiving with prayer is natural and frequent; cf. 1 Thess. i. 2; Rom. i. 8 f.; Phil. i. 3 f.; Col. i. 3; Ephes. i. 16.

16 Now our Lord Jesus Christ himself, and God even our Father, which hath loved us, and hath given us everlasting consolation, and good hope through grace, 17 Comfort your hearts, and stablish you in every good word and work.

As in i. 11, 12 and 1 Thess. iii. 11, 12, v. 23, 24, exhortation to the converts passes into prayer for them. This, as Chrysostom points out, is real help. And there is again the emphasis thrown upon the need of Divine assistance. Exhortation and teaching will have little effect, unless they have the support of our Lord and our heavenly Father. *Satis innuit quam parum valeant exhortationes, nisi Deus corda intus moveat et efficiat* (Calvin).

16 Now may our Lord Jesus Christ *Himself*, and God our Father who loved us in sending His Son to redeem us, and gave us immeasurable comfort and encouragement for the present moment and good hope for the future, all which was pure grace without merit of ours,
17 comfort *your* hearts and stablish them in every good work that you do and every good word that you say.

16. **Now may . . . Himself]** As in 1 Thess. iii. 11 and v. 23, the prayer begins with an emphatic pronoun and a particle which is mainly one of transition to a new subject, but partly one of contrast to what has just been said, *Αὐτὸς δέ*. The contrast is with 'our word or letter'; we may plant, but it is God alone Who gives the increase. Four times in these two letters the missionaries call attention to this supreme fact; 1 Thess. iii. 11, v. 23; 2 Thess. ii. 16, iii. 16. As in 1 Thess. iii. 11, both the Father and the Son are mentioned as the source of benefits, and there the usual order of the two Persons is observed. Here, as in 2 Cor.

xiii. 13, the Son is placed first. The reason here may be that the Apostle is still thinking of 'the glory of our Lord Jesus Christ' (*v.* 14). In any case, he seems to see no incongruity in mentioning Christ before the Father. The expression Θεὸς ὁ πατὴρ ἡμῶν occurs nowhere else.

who loved us] This probably refers to the Father only (cf. Gal. i. 1), but the singular (ὁ ἀγαπήσας ἡμᾶς) does not prove this. See E. A. Abbott, *Johannine Vocabulary*, p. 260. The aorist clearly refers to some great manifestation in the past with which Christians are familiar, and the work of redemption is almost certainly meant. Cf. Jn. iii. 16, where loving and giving are combined; also Rom. v. 8, viii. 37–39; Gal. ii. 20; Eph. v. 2, 25. 'Loveth us and loosed us' is a similar combination Rev. i. 5.

immeasurable comfort and encouragement] The expression is remarkable,—παράκλησιν αἰωνίαν, which the A.V. renders 'everlasting consolation,' and the R.V. 'eternal comfort.' The A.V. wavers in its renderings of αἰώνιος between 'everlasting' and 'eternal'; the R.V. is constant with 'eternal,' which is much to be preferred. 'Eternal' is the opposite of 'temporal'; and 'temporal' means what can be measured by periods of time, while 'eternal' means what cannot be so measured. See on i. 9. But 'eternal' is not quite suitable here, for the point seems to be that the Divine παράκλησις utterly transcends the consolations of this world; our transitory afflictions cannot exhaust it. It is never insufficient. It turns sorrow into joy. Neither 'consolation' nor 'comfort' is quite adequate. It includes the ideas of comfort and encouragement, and we need both words. See on 1 Thess. iii. 2, 7 and iv. 18.

It is seldom that adjectives in -ιος have a feminine termination, and, excepting here and Heb. ix. 12, αἰώνιος in N.T. has only two terminations. Num. xxv. 13 we have διαθήκη αἰωνία, and Jer. xx. 17, συλλήψεως αἰωνίας.

good hope] 'Good' both here and in the next verse is too vague for ἀγαθός, but it is difficult to find a better word that will fit both places. Perhaps 'solid' might serve; 'solid hope,' 'solid deeds and words.' The hope is not baseless or deceptive ; it is sound in itself and beneficial in its effects. Cf. 1 Thess. iii. 6, iv. 13, v. 15 ; Jas. i. 17. 'The hope of good things to come' (Theodoret) is not the meaning. 'Good hope' is a set expression both in English and in Greek.

pure grace] The addition ἐν χάριτι belongs to the whole sentence, 'who loved us, etc.' We have no deserts to plead as a claim on God's love and benefits ; they are free gifts, not payments. See on i. 12.

17. **comfort your hearts**] Give them calm after the unhealthy excitement respecting the Advent. As in 1 Thess. iii. 11, although both the Son and the Father are nominatives, the verb is singular, 3rd pers. aor. opt. "There is probably no instance in St. Paul of a plural adjective or verb, where the two Persons of the Godhead are mentioned" (Lightfoot). The 'heart' in Scripture includes the moral elements as well as the emotional ; it is 'the hidden man,' as seen by God, and the sphere of religious experience ; 1 Thess. ii. 4, iii. 13 ; Col. ii. 2 ; Eph. vi. 22 ; 1 Pet. iii. 4. It is precisely there that we receive consolation and encouragement. Hastings' *D.C.G.* and *D.A.C.*, art. 'Heart.' 'Your' is emphatic.

and stablish them] 'Them' is not expressed in the true text. Some inferior authorities, followed by A.V., insert 'you.' But 'your hearts' is the acc. after both 'comfort' and 'stablish.' 'Stablish' (στηρίξαι), 'strengthen,' or 'confirm,' means make you secure against being 'shaken' or 'troubled' (*v.* 2), and thus made to fall away from holiness. In these two verbs we have the true optative, expressing a wish, as also in iii. 5, 16. In N.T. it is almost always in the 3rd. pers. sing. The one exception is Philem. 20. Burton § 175, 176.

We have the same verb 1 Thess. iii. 2, 13 ; Rom. i. 11, xvi. 25 ; and the same idea expressed by βεβαιοῦν 1 Cor. i. 8 ; 2 Cor. i. 21 ; θεμελιοῦν Eph. iii. 17 ; Col. i. 23 ; σθενοῦν 1 Pet. v. 10. "This frequent reference to the need of στηριγμός in Christian communities planted in the heart of a heathen population will readily explain itself to those who are familiar with the history of Missions" (Swete on Rev. iii. 2).

With στηρίξαι cf. στηρίξει iii. 3: in Lk. xxii. 32 and Rev. iii. 2 we have στήρισον, cf. Jer. xvii. 5; Ezek. xx. 46; 1 Macc. xiv. 14.

in every good work and every good word] The A.V. is certainly wrong with 'every good word and work.' Such is the usual order of these two substantives (Rom. xv. 18; 2 Cor. x. 11; Col. iii. 17), and inferior authorities have the usual order here. Cf. Lk. xxiii. 51, xxiv. 19. The point here is 'not only in acts, which are all-important, but also in words, which are less so.' 'Every' and 'good' belong to both substantives. Chrysostom and Calvin are obviously in error in interpreting 'good word' as 'sound doctrine.' It means every kind and beneficent word, for which there is opportunity daily and hourly for soothing and aiding others.

The whole of this passage breathes the Pauline spirit, as we find it Rom. viii. 17, 29, 37–39; Gal. ii. 20. It also illustrates the spirit of these primitive Churches in their infancy. *Tout cela était spontané, sans contrainte, et pourtant des petites associations étaient solides comme le fer* (Renan, *Saint Paul*, p. 237).

iii. 1-16. CHEERING AND COMMANDING

This third main division of the Epistle consists of three unequal sections, between which there is a manifest pause, 1–5, 6–15, and 16. In the first two we have Exhortation, in the last Prayer. But, as was stated at the outset, it is not easy to find accurately appropriate headings for each portion of this Epistle.

iii. 1–5. Request, Encouragement, and Prayer

The exhortation in this section differs considerably from that in the next. Its object is, not to admonish the Thessalonians respecting evils which exist among them, but to ask them to remember the writers in their prayers. This request had been made in the earlier letter (v. 25). It is now repeated with a statement as to the direction which the intercessions should take. Just as the request in ii. 1, 2 forms an introduction to the instructions respecting the Day of the Lord, so these first two verses form an introduction to the instructions respecting the disorderly.

iii. 1, 2. *Request.*

1 Finally, brethren, pray for us, that the word of the Lord may have *free* course, and be glorified, even as it is with you: 2 And that we may be delivered from unreasonable and wicked men: for all men have not faith.

The Apostle, like his Master, prays for himself and his disciples; and he charges them to pray for themselves and for others. But he also does, what Christ nowhere does; he asks them to pray for himself. This difference is not pointed out in Scripture, but it is significant; the Lord needs no man's intercessions. Here, after praying for the Thessalonians, it is natural that he and his fellow-workers should ask the Thessalonians to pray for them. There is a similar sequence in 1 Thess. v. 23–25, and in each case the request is accompanied by the affectionate address, 'Brethren.' St. Paul often desires the prayers of those to whom he writes; Rom. xv. 30, 31; Eph. vi. 19; Col. iv. 3; cf. 2 Cor. i. 11; Phil. i. 19; Philem. 22.

1 We have something more to add to our prayers for you: we beg that you, Brethren, will *make us the subject of your prayers.* In particular, ask that the word of the Lord may run the very same swift course and have the very same glorious reception in the case of other hearers as has already been the case in reference to yourselves. And, that this may be so, ask that we may be delivered from those perverse and evil men, who are even now at work against us. And it must be so, for alas! by no means all share our faith.

1. **We have something more to add]** Like 1 Thess. iv. 1, this new division opens with an expression (τὸ λοιπόν)

which implies that, although the writer has his conclusion in sight, yet it has not been reached. There is perhaps no appreciable difference between λοιπόν (1 Thess. iv. 1; 1 Cor. i. 16; 2 Cor. xiii. 11) and τὸ λοιπόν (2 Thess. iii. 1; Phil. iii. 1): but possibly λοιπόν is rather more colloquial. A.V. and R.V. have 'Finally' for both forms, and the Vulgate nearly always has *de caetero* for both. 'Finally' is not quite satisfactory, because in 1 Thess. iv. 1 and Phil. iii. 1 the expression is distant from the actual conclusion of the Epistle. This is so completely the case in 1 Cor. i. 16 that both A.V. and R.V. have 'Besides' instead of 'Finally.' 'For the rest' might serve here and elsewhere. In no case does the expression intimate that what follows is comparatively of slight importance. The very reverse is the fact here. This chapter contains one of the chief objects of the letter.

make us the subject of your prayers] Here προσεύχεσθε precedes ἀδελφοί, and therefore is more emphatic than in 1 Thess. v. 25; 'not merely hold fast our doctrine (ii. 15), but *pray* for us.' In both cases, as in Col. iv. 3, we have the indefinite περί, instead of the more usual and more expressive ὑπέρ. Possibly 'think of us in your prayers' seemed to be a more modest way of putting the request than 'pray on our behalf.' See Lightfoot on Gal. i. 4. Elsewhere we have ὑπέρ: Phil. i 4; Col. i. 9, iv. 12; 1 Tim. ii. 2; cf. Mt. v. 44; Acts viii. 24.

In particular] The details are twofold; that their preaching of the Gospel may have a rapid and triumphant course, and that the Apostle and his colleagues may be preserved from their outrageous opponents. Theodoret remarks that the request is only apparently twofold, because it is by the defeat of the evil men that the Gospel has a free course. That, however, was not the only reason for desiring deliverance from such men. Each detail has an appendix. the one respecting the reception of the faith by the Thessalonians, the other respecting its rejection by others.

ask that] For ἵνα after verbs of praying and asking cf. i. 11 and 1 Thess. iv. 1, and see Lightfoot on Phil. i. 9 and Col. i. 9. In such cases the idea of purpose is almost lost in that of purport. Here both the verbs which follow are in the present tense; the rapid progress and the glorious fruit are to be lasting.

the word of the Lord may run the very same swift course] This is possibly a reminiscence of Ps. cxlvii. 15, 'His word runneth very swiftly.' Reminiscence of the Psalms are probable enough; their liturgical use in the synagogues made them familiar. But St. Paul is so fond of metaphors taken from athletic sports, that there is no need to look for a parallel in the O.T. Cf. Rom. ix. 16; 1 Cor. ix. 24–26; Gal. ii. 2, v. 7; Phil. ii. 16. See Deissmann, *St. Paul*, p. 214.

'The word of the Lord' is Christ's message of Good-tidings. That 'the Lord' here means Christ, as usually with St. Paul, is evident from *vv.* 3, 4, 5. This is another illustration, and a remarkable one, of the facility with which the first Christians transferred to Christ what is said in the O.T. of God. See on 1 Thess. iv. 15.

the very same] Not simply ὡς, but καθώς, as in i. 3 and very often in 1 Thess.*

glorious reception] 'Be glorified' (δοξάζηται) means be glorified as the Gentiles of Pisidian Antioch glorified it (Acts xiii. 48), by receiving it joyfully, believing it, and living in accordance with it. Such converts 'adorn the doctrine of God our Saviour,' Tit. ii. 10; cf. Phil. ii. 15, 16. See Sanday and Headlam on Rom. i. 21.

in reference to yourselves] This is not quite the same use of πρὸς ὑμᾶς as in ii. 5, iii. 10, and 1 Thess. iii. 4. There it has reference to residence among the Thessalonians; here it indicates the influence of the word of the Lord in relation to them. Its influence over them had been rapid and triumphant, and the Apostle tactfully reminds them of this. But his meaning is not, 'Do not think that the word has been as triumphant as it has been with you' (Bengel), but, 'Having begun well, be all the more careful against slackness and backsliding.'

* The clause καθὼς καί shows that 'run' means 'move *swiftly*,' rather than 'unencumbered by obstacles superimposed by adversaries.' The word had had swift course at Thessalonica, but it had been bitterly opposed; it had not been 'untrammelled' (Way).

2. **that we may be delivered** etc.] Of course if the outrageous enemies of the three preachers were victorious, there would be grievous hindrance to the spread of the Gospel. But there may be more in the request than that. The bitter hostility which had driven them from Philippi, Thessalonica, and Beroea was now rendering life in Corinth almost intolerable. The change from the present tenses in *v.* 1 to the aorist (ῥυσθῶμεν) here indicates a definite persecution. See Rom. xv. 31; Acts xx. 3, 22, 23, xxi. 11. Even independently of the hindrance to their work as preachers, they would long to be freed from this trouble and danger; and they might well ask their converts to pray for their deliverance, especially converts who knew from experience the affliction caused by malignant persecution. 'Delivered *from*' (ἀπό) is as in the Lord's Prayer; in 1 Thess. i. 10 we have 'out of' (ἐκ). 'Rescue' might in most places be a better rendering of ῥύεσθαι (Rom. vii. 24; 2 Cor. i. 10; Col. i. 13); but it is important to preserve the resemblance to the Lord's Prayer.

those perverse and evil men] For 'perverse' (ἀτόπων) A.V. and R.V. have 'unreasonable,' which is inadequate. The word means 'out-of-place,' 'out-of-the question,' and so 'outrageous,' whether of persons or things. Elsewhere in N.T. it is used of things; Lk. xxiii. 41; Acts xxv. 5, xxviii. 6; and in each case A.V. has a different rendering,—'something amiss,' 'wickedness,' 'harm.'* In O.T. also it is neuter; Job xxvii. 6, xxxvi. 2 (*v. l.* ἄδικα and ἄνομα); etc. See Wetstein here, Lk. xxiii. 41, 2, and Acts xxviii. 6. Both adjectives are words of strong meaning, and the article (τῶν ἀτόπων καὶ πονηρῶν ἀνθρώπων) shows that some definite group of assailants is meant: they are there and are at work.

for alas!] The 'for' (γάρ) indicates how natural it is that Christian missionaries should be virulently opposed at Corinth: there are many fanatical Jews there, and to them

* Vulg. has *importuni* here, *malum* and *crimen* in Lk. and Acts. That 'out-of-place' means 'homeless vagabonds,' is a curious suggestion, accepted now by no one.

the Gospel is anathema. *Sunagogas Judaeorum fontes persecutionum* (Tert. *Scorp.* 10). See on ii. 7 and iii. 7 for γάρ.

by no means all share our faith] A mournful understatement, with perhaps a touch of irony; οὐ γὰρ πάντων ἡ πίστις. Wetstein quotes the well-known proverb, Οὐ παντὸς ἀνδρὸς ἐς Κόρινθόν ἐσθ' ὁ πλοῦς, *Non cuivis homini contingit adire Corinthum.* Cf. τὸ γνῶναι ἑαυτὸν χαλεπόν τι, καὶ οὐχὶ παντός, Plato, *Alcib.* p. 429 A. For similar understatements cf. Rom. i. 28, x. 16; 1 Cor. xi. 22; Philem. 11. Certainly not here, and very rarely elsewhere, does πίστις mean 'faithfulness' or 'fidelity,' and πιστός in *v.* 3 is no evidence that it does. '*The* faith' has the same meaning here as in Acts vi. 7 and Rom. xi. 20 and Eph. iv. 13. See Robertson and Plummer on 1 Cor. xvi. 13. Those who do not possess it are not faithless Christians but rank unbelievers; this is the common meaning of ἄπιστοι in 1 and 2 Cor. For the possessive genitive cf. 2 Cor. ii. 3 and Heb. v. 14.

3, 4. *Encouragement.*

From the depressing want of faith in so many among mankind we pass to the absolute faithfulness of Christ, and this is a very cheering thought.

[3] But the Lord is faithful, who shall stablish you, and keep you from evil. [4] And we have confidence in the Lord touching you, that ye both do, and will do the things which we command you.

St. Paul is fond of playing upon words, whether through different shades of meaning or similarity of sound,—in particular, alliteration with the letter π. See Plummer on 2 Cor. iv. 15, ix. 8, x. 6, 13. Here πίστις suggests πιστός. In much the same way in 2 Tim. ii. 13 ἀπιστοῦμεν, of man's *unbelief* with regard to God, suggests πιστός, of God's *faithfulness* with regard to man. See on i. 10, where τοῖς πιστεύσασιν is followed by an awkward parenthesis introducing ἐπιστεύθη.

[3] **But, although there are many who reject the Christian faith,**

yet assuredly the Lord Jesus Christ *is* always found faithful. He will not only establish you in a sure place, but will keep you safe from the assaults of the evil one. [4] But it is not because we think that you are failing that we assure you of the Divine protection; it is because we are so certain that the Lord Jesus is with you that we rely upon you, confident that you are acting, and will continue to act, in accordance with the charges that we give.

3. **The Lord**] As usual, this means Christ; see on *v.* 1. Some witnesses have 'God' for 'Lord.' Similar confusion is found in *v.* 16.

is always found faithful] He is always exhibiting fidelity to His word and office; He is to be trusted. The otherwise superfluous ἐστιν (1 Cor. i. 9, x. 13; 2 Cor. i. 18) is inserted for emphasis. Fidelity to His word is in O.T. a special attribute of God; Deut. vii. 8, 9; Is. xlix. 7; and it is here transferred to Christ.

There is no need to suppose that this alludes to a letter from the Thessalonians in which they excused their misconduct on the ground that the Tempter was too strong for them. See on i. 3, 11.

establish you] See on ii. 17. The use of the verb there may have suggested its use here, as Theodore of Mopsuestia seems to have thought.

will keep you safe from] The same verb and construction (φυλάσσειν ἀπό) occurs Lk. xii. 15; 1 Jn. v. 21; Ps. cxl. (cxli.) 9. Our Lord speaks of His action in this respect in His High-Priestly prayer Jn. xvii. 12. This verse, like 1 Thess. v. 24, has the ring of a magnificent confidence.

the assaults of the evil one] There will always be discussion as to the exact meaning of the words here and in the Lord's Prayer, of which these words are possibly an echo, ἀπὸ τοῦ πονηροῦ. Is the adjective masculine or neuter? 'evil one' or 'evil'? The A.V. has 'evil' here and Mt. vi. 13; also Lk. xi. 4, where the clause is an interpolation. The R.V. has 'evil *one*' here and Mt. vi. 13, with 'evil' in the margin. The overwhelming weight of modern scholarship is in favour of the masculine in the Lord's Prayer and therefore here. In the N.T. there are only two absolutely certain instances of the neuter (Lk. vi. 45; Rom. xii. 9) against ten certain instances of the masculine (Mt. v. 37, xiii. 19, 38, 49; Eph. vi. 16; 1 Jn. ii. 13, 14, iii. 12, v. 18, 19). Jewish formularies favour the masculine, and the Greek Fathers unanimously adopt the masculine in the Lord's Prayer. Even without the high probability derived from the parallel in the Prayer, there is good reason for believing that 'the evil one' is right here. Satan has been mentioned as the inspirer of the wickedness and deceit connected with the Lawless One (ii. 9), and the Thessalonians have just been asked to pray that their teachers may be delivered from the evil men. It is probable therefore that we here have a reference to him who is the inspirer of such men and their leader,—*improborum caput*, as Calvin calls him. Moreover, 'the evil one' is the appropriate antithesis of 'the Lord.' As to St. Paul's usage elsewhere, there is Eph. vi. 16, where τοῦ πονηροῦ must mean 'the evil one.' It is unconvincing to urge that 'establish you and keep you safe from the evil' corresponds with 'establish you in every good word and work,' and that, as 'word and work' are impersonal, 'evil' must be impersonal. Nevertheless, neither rendering can be proved to be correct, and the question remains open. See Lightfoot *ad loc.* and *On a Fresh Revision*, pp. 269 ff.; also F. H. Chase, *The Lord's Prayer in the Early Church, Texts and Studies*, I. 3, pp. 70 ff.

4. **But**] The δέ implies that the writers have no distrust of the loyalty of their converts.

that the Lord Jesus is with you] It is 'in the Lord' (1 Thess. iii. 8, iv. 1, v. 12; Rom. xiv. 14, etc.), that is, 'in Christ,' that the writers hold their confident reliance upon the fidelity of the Thessalonians. He inspires the trust. All that the Apostle thinks or does has for him a religious aspect. It is all 'in the Lord' or 'in Christ.' This Epistle and Titus are the only letters in which the expression 'in Christ' does not occur: but we here have its equivalent. The accusative (πεποίθαμεν ἐφ' ὑμᾶς) is unusual; but cf. 2 Cor. ii. 3 and Gal. v. 10; also οἱ πεποιθότες ἐπὶ Κύριον Ps. cxxiv. (cxxv.) 1. Elsewhere we have the more classical dative.

the charges that we give] Or, 'the things which we command.' It is words of command from persons in authority that the writers issue, not mere requests or suggestions. Such is the meaning of παραγγέλλομεν. See on 1 Thess. iv. 2, 11. Some commentators take the verb here as anticipating the same word in *v.* 6. This is unlikely, for *vv.* 6–14 refer to evils which are harming the Thessalonians, and which they are charged to remedy. The Apostle could hardly say with express reference to these evils that the converts are doing (ποιεῖτε) what they are charged to do. Others take παραγγέλλομεν here as meaning the charge just given; 'Pray for us. But we are sure that you do pray for us, and will do so.' This is less unlikely. But it seems better to make the reference quite general, covering all charges which have been given or may be given. With his usual tact and tenderness the Apostle desires to give the Thessalonians full credit for their good conduct and good-will, and he does this before finding fault and giving fresh charges. Cf. 1 Thess. i. 3–9, ii. 13, iii. 6–9, iv. 1, 9, 10, v. 11. Vulg. has *praecipio* here, but in 6, 10, 12 *denuntio*.

Owing to the doubt as to the charges to which παραγγέλλομεν refers, the text has become confused. Among other variations καὶ ἐποιήσατε has been interpolated before καὶ ποιεῖτε καὶ ποιήσετε,—'ye have done, and are doing, and will do the things which we command. The original reading seems to be καὶ ποιεῖτε καὶ ποιήσετε. The first καί, if genuine, must not be joined to the protasis—'that what we command and ye do, ye will continue to do.' 'That what we command, ye both do and will continue to do' is the meaning.

5. *Prayer.*

[5] And the Lord direct your hearts into the love of God, and into the patient waiting for Christ.

Before laying any further commands upon the converts the writers pray for them once more. The Divine blessing is needed to secure the desired result.

[5] Yes, we have full confidence in you ; but may the Lord Jesus direct *your* hearts into the love which has been manifested towards us by God, and into the hopeful endurance which has been manifested by the Christ.

5. **But may the Lord**] The δέ is 'But,' rather than 'And'; it looks back to πεποίθαμεν. 'We confidently rely on your good intentions; *but* we pray that the Lord may guide you.' 'The Lord' has the usual Pauline meaning of Christ. Basil (*De Spir. Sanct.*, 21) and other Greek commentators think that the Holy Spirit is meant; but that would be against all N.T. usage.

direct your hearts] Remove all that might hinder them from this movement. Cf. 1 Thess. iii. 11 and Lk. i. 79, the only other passages in N.T. in which κατευθύνειν occurs, and always with the meaning of Divine Providence guiding human action. In LXX it is very frequent in this sense. E. A. Abbott, *Johannine Grammar*, p. 84. 'Your' looks back to 'rely upon you' in *v.* 4, and is emphatic.

into the love] So as to absorb it and exhibit it in word and work. It is difficult to decide whether 'the love of God' (ἡ ἀγάπη τοῦ Θεοῦ) here means His love for us or our love for Him; and it does not settle this question to notice that 'the patience of Christ' must mean the endurance which He exhibited in His life and in His death. The one genitive may be subjective and the other objective. In 2 Cor. xiii. 13, although the first is subjective, the second or the third or both may be objective. It is probable that here both are of one kind, and both subjective; but this is not certain. Bengel makes both objective. Lightfoot, in his very full note, thinks that in both cases both meanings are combined. See last note on ii. 13. See Deissmann on "the mystic genitive," *St. Paul*, p. 141.

The meaning of ὑπομονή is not doubtful; it is uniform in N.T. Here it is neither 'patient waiting for Christ' (A.V.), nor 'stedfastness for His sake,' but 'His hopeful endurance of opposition.' The prayer is that the converts may endure patiently and hopefully as He did. In LXX ὑπομονή is the rendering of Hebrew words denoting *hope*, which is the basis of pious endurance, viz. the sure hope that God will make the trouble fruitful. See on i. 4. Cf. Rev. iii. 10, *τῆς ὑπομονῆς μου*, 'the endurance practised by Me'; xiii. 10, xiv. 12, 'the endurance practised by the Saints'; Ign. *Rom.* x. 3, *ἔρρωσθε εἰς τέλος ἐν ὑπομονῇ Ἰ. Χριστοῦ.* This is an introduction to what follows. Those who administer discipline must have love and patience.

The article before *Χριστοῦ* must be noted; 'the patient Christ,' 'the suffering Servant' of Jehovah (Is. liii.).

6–15. Reproof and Instruction

This hortatory paragraph deals with one of the two main subjects of the letter, the purpose of which is two-fold; first and foremost, to correct erroneous ideas about the Second Advent; secondly, to correct certain evil habits which probably were largely the result of these erroneous ideas. This second object is the subject of these ten verses. The exhortation is of two kinds; reproof of the idle and disorderly members (6–12), and instruction to the loyal members as to dealing with disobedience, if it should occur (13–15).

These verses give us clearer ideas as to the situation in Thessalonica when 1 Thess. was written than we get from 1 Thess. They reflect "an intimate and firsthand acquaintance with the situation pre-supposed by 1 Thess. iv. 11, 12, v. 14" (Frame). This does not look like the work of a forger. See the excellent remarks of Cassian in Book X. of the *Institutes*, vii.–xvi., *Of the Spirit of Accidie*, on the difference of tone between 1 and 2 Thess., as illustrated by these verses.

The paragraph is also "important as bearing on the degree of authority which the Apostle exercised. It seems to have been partly official and partly moral, springing from what the Apostle had done for the Church, yet also claimed by him as a right. In any voluntary society the enforcement of such an authority must have depended on feeling and opinion. There was no way of enforcement in the last resort but the separation of the society itself from the individual" (Jowett).

6–12. *Reproof of the Idle and Disorderly.*

6 Now we command you, brethren, in the Name of our Lord Jesus
Christ, that ye withdraw yourselves from every brother that walketh
disorderly, and not after the tradition which he received from us.
7 For yourselves know how ye ought to follow us: for we behaved
not ourselves disorderly among you, 8 Neither did we eat any man's
bread for nought: but we wrought with labour and travail night
and day, that we might not be chargeable to any of you. 9 Not
because we have not power, but to make ourselves an ensample unto
you to follow us. 10 For even when we were with you, this we com-
manded you, that if any would not work, neither should he eat.
11 For we hear that there are some which walk among you disorderly,
working not at all, but are busybodies. 12 Now them that are such,
we command, and exhort by our Lord Jesus Christ, that with quiet-
ness they work, and eat their own bread.

Souvent Paul était impérieux, et faisait sentir son autorité avec un ascendant qui nous choque. Il commande, il blâme durement; il parle de lui-même avec assurance et se propose de modèle sans hésiter . . . Le mobile de son zèle était un amour des âmes en quelque sorte infini (Renan, *Saint Paul*, pp. 236 f.).

**6 Now, with a view to the fulfilment of this prayer, Brethren, we
issue a word of command to you, which we give not only on our
own authority, but on that of our Lord Jesus Christ,—and as being
brethren and His subjects you are bound to be united in obedience.
You must keep yourselves from associating with *any* brother who is
leading a disorderly life and not one that is in accordance with the
Divine rule which was transmitted by us and received from us by you.
7 You see the reasonableness of this command, for *out of your own
experience* you know in what manner you ought to live so as to
imitate us. You know this, because there was nothing disorderly
in our life when we were among you. 8 Nor yet were we idle; for
we did not get from any one the bread that we ate, without earning
it. On the contrary, in toil and travail, night and day, we worked
so as not to lay an unnecessary burden on any of you. 9 We did this,
not because we have no right to maintenance; but we did it in order
to give *ourselves* to you as an example in which you might imitate us.**

10 And besides giving you an example, you know that, when we were with you, we repeatedly gave you a command to *this* effect, If any one does not choose to work, neither let him eat. 11 We repeat this now, for reports are reaching us that there are certain persons leading among you disorderly lives, who work not at all at their own business, but are busily employed in doing nothing. 12 Now it is people of this kind that we command and exhort in the Lord Jesus Christ, that with quietness working at their business they eat the bread which they have *earned*.

6. **Now, with a view to the fulfilment of this prayer**] The δέ marks the transition to a new topic, which is slightly in contrast to what precedes. 'And' would give no contrast; 'But' would make it too strong. See on ii. 1 and 16. Evidently the Apostle does not expect to revisit them soon.

Brethren] This softens the severity of what is coming (ii. 1, 15; 1 Thess. iv. 1, 13), and may serve to remind them that in a congregation of brethren these differences and disorders ought not to occur. Moreover, the missionaries are writing as brothers to brothers in the authority of One who is above both.

we issue a word of command] This is the opening word of the paragraph—*παραγγέλλομεν*. See above on *v.* 4. What was there said of the preachers' words in general is now repeated of the special precepts which follow. See on 1 Thess. iv. 2.

to you] To the sober majority, who are not idle busybodies.

on that of the Lord Jesus] The writers have sufficient authority of their own, but it is not claimed on personal grounds; and they can appeal to something much higher. This statement, placed in advance of the commands, prepares us for a matter of grave import. Cf. 1 Thess. iv. 2 and see Robertson and Plummer on 1 Cor. v. 4. Like 'Brethren,' it may serve to remind the recipients of what is required of those who have Christ as their Lord. Again we have an expression (*ἐν ὀνόματι τοῦ Κυρίου*) which in the O.T. is used of Jehovah (Exod. v. 23; Lev. xix. 12; Deut. xviii. 22; Jer. xi. 21; etc) transferred readily to Christ

(1 Cor. vi. 11; Eph. v. 20; Col. iii. 17, etc.). See on i. 12 and 1 Thess. iv. 1.

The injunctions which follow are more definite and stringent than those in 1 Thess. The need for them has become more urgent. All this is natural and in favour of genuineness.

You must keep yourselves from] The phrase is remarkable; στέλλεσθαι ὑμᾶς ἀπό. Both στέλλειν and στέλλεσθαι are used of girding up one's robe; and it is possible that στέλλεσθαι comes to mean 'draw back' because gathering one's dress closely to one sometimes expresses disgust or displeasure. In any case στέλλω 'I tighten' easily becomes 'I check,' and στέλλομαι 'I check myself' easily becomes 'I draw back.' See Wetstein on 2 Cor. viii. 20, the only other passage in N.T. in which the verb occurs. In Wisd. xiv. 1 and 2 Macc. v. 1 it is used of 'setting sail,' 'starting.' But the meaning is certain, in whatever way it may be reached. 'You must withdraw from,' 'keep aloof from'; *subtrahatis vos* (Vulg. here; in 2 Cor. viii. 20 *devitantes*). Ambrosiaster has *secerni vos.* In *De singul. cleric.* 36 (Hartel's Cyprian, II. p. 212), *ut separetis vos.* See Lightfoot on ὑπέστελλε Gal. ii. 12. See Westcott on Heb. x. 38.

any brother] There are to be no exceptions even in the case of those who in other respects seem to be living correctly; παντός is emphatic. The case is similar to the one in 1 Cor. v. 11; but there 'who bears the name of a brother' implies that such grave offenders have forfeited the name of Christian. Here the condemnation is less stern. The disorderly people are to be left severely alone, partly that they may realize how serious their misbehaviour is, and partly to prevent other Christians from being corrupted. *Ordo mendicantium non est ordo, sed gravat rempublicam ipsam* (Bengel). Nothing is said about excommunication, but the strict observance of this command would involve exclusion from the Lord's Supper.

leading a disorderly life] The evil had been touched upon 1 Thess. v. 14; 'admonish the disorderly,' τοὺς ἀτάκτους, those who do not keep the ranks, but are lax, slovenly, and addicted to deliberate loafing. Here there are people whose general life is of this character, ἀτάκτως περιπατοῦντες. The common view that this disorderly idleness was the result of the belief that the end of the world had begun is probable enough, as experience in later ages has shown. But the connexion is neither stated nor clearly implied in the letter. Lightfoot quotes the concluding words of Germanicus to his troops respecting the mutiny of two legions (Tac. *Ann.* i. 43); "Stand aloof from contamination, and separate the mutinous (*turbidos*) from among you. That will be a pledge for repentance; that will be a guarantee of your loyalty." Milligan quotes papyri in which ἀτακτεῖν is used of playing truant and being idle. Frame, in *Essays in Modern Theology* (dedicated to C. A. Briggs on his 70th birthday, 1911), pp. 191–206, argues strongly in favour of Rutherford's rendering of οἱ ἄτακτοι and ἀτακτεῖν as 'the loafers' and 'to loaf.' In letters addressed to a Church which consisted largely of working men the words are not inappropriate. Nevertheless 'disorderly' is etymologically closer to the Greek word, and is free from all flavour of slang.

transmitted by us and received from us by you] *Παράδοσιν* implies that it did not originate with the writers. It was a 'tradition' which they themselves had received from above and had handed on. See on ii. 15. 'Received by *you*' ought possibly to be 'received by *them*.' The reading is uncertain. There are five variations. '*He* received' (A.V.) has little claim to consideration; but two other readings are well attested; '*ye* received' (παρελάβετε) and '*they* received' (παρελάβοσαν). No copyist would deliberately alter παρελάβετε into παρελάβοσαν, which is less easy and is also an unusual and rare form; * the converse alteration might be made. But παρελάβοσαν might be caused by accidental confusion. If 'they received' be adopted,

* Cf. εἴχοσαν Jn. xv. 22, 24; ἐδολιοῦσαν Rom. iii. 13 from the LXX; ἤλθοσαν Ps. lxxviii. 1. Here and 1 Thess. ii. 13, iv. 1, we have παρά repeated after a verb compounded with παρά, and this is rare. A. T. Robertson, *Gr.*, pp. 335 f., 560.

'they' refers to 'every brother.' For 'walking' or 'living in accordance with' (περιπατεῖν κατά) cf. Rom. viii. 4, xiv. 15; 1 Cor. iii. 3; 2 Cor. x. 2. The metaphor is a frequent Hebraism.

Chrysostom can hardly be right in limiting the 'tradition' to meaning the *example* set by the writers. It may include that, but it means chiefly their teaching as to Christian life whether by word of mouth or by letter. Cf. *v.* 10 and 1 Thess. iv. 11.

The next three verses (7–9) are similar to 1 Cor. ix. 12, 15 and 2 Cor. xi. 7–9.

7. **for**] The γάρ implies that what follows explains what precedes; their knowledge explains the charge to keep aloof from the idlers. Such a charge was needed, for disorderly conduct is so unlike the pattern which the missionaries had set before them. Three reasons for the charge are given; one here, another in *v.* 10 (καὶ γάρ), and a third in *v.* 11 (γάρ).

you know] Again and again in 1 Thess. the writers appeal to their converts' own experience; 1 Thess. i. 5, ii. 1, 2, 5, etc. Here αὐτοί is emphatic as in 1 Thess. ii. 1, iii. 3, v. 2. They do not need to be informed.

in what manner you ought to live in order to imitate us] The Greek is condensed; 'how you ought to imitate us,' πῶς δεῖ μιμεῖσθαι ἡμᾶς, where 'how' refers to 'imitate' and not to 'ought.' It indicates the direction which the imitation must take, not the ground of the obligation. 'To *follow* us' (A.V.) is too vague, and 'follow' is required for ἀκολουθεῖν, which is frequent in N.T.

because there was nothing disorderly] They know, because they saw the way in which the missionaries lived, for they lived in their midst. We have here another understatement, not mournful, as in *v.* 2, but modest.

8. **Nor yet**] There was another thing besides undisciplined behaviour from which the missionaries abstained, viz. sponging upon other people for their daily bread. They 'did not eat bread *gratis* (δωρεάν) at the hands of any one,' 'did not take free meals from any one' (Moffatt). 'Eat

any man's bread' (A.V.) is inaccurate. Δωρεάν occurs Mt. x. 8; Rom. iii. 24; 2 Cor. xi. 7; Rev. xxi. 6, xxii. 17, and is frequent in LXX. From '*gratis*, for nothing' we easily pass to 'without cause' and 'uselessly'; Jn. xv. 25; Gal. ii. 21. 'Eat bread' means more than an occasional meal; it implies sustenance generally. See Briggs on Ps. xiv. 4 and Skinner on Gen. iii. 19.

On the contrary] As in ii. 12. For οὐκ . . . οὐδὲ . . . ἀλλά cf. 1 Thess. ii. 3, 4.

in toil and travail] We have the same combination (κόπος and μόχθος) 1 Thess. ii. 9 and 2 Cor. xi. 27, and it is not necessary to distinguish the two words any more than to distinguish 'toil' from 'travail.' In LXX we commonly have κόπος καὶ πόνος, sing. or plur. Cf. 'toil and trouble,' 'toil and moil.' So far from living on others, the preachers worked hard to maintain themselves. Acts xviii. 3 leaves us in doubt about St. Paul's handicraft. Did he weave material for tent making? or only cut it out and stitch it together? And what was the material? Cloth (*cilicium*) or leather? About the way in which Silvanus and Timothy maintained themselves we know nothing. His enemies said, that like other impostors, the Apostle preached to fill his pockets. It was important to give no handle for this, but be independent of his converts. He was not afraid of being tempted to shape his preaching with a view to profit. While in Thessalonica he accepted help from the Philippians (Phil. iv. 16). That did not endanger his independence at Thessalonica. See on 2 Cor. xi. 9.

The similarity of this verse to 1 Thess. ii. 9 is regarded by some as evidence that this letter is a forgery, partly based on 1 Thess. But the writer of 1 Thess., when discussing the same subject a few months later, would be likely to use similar language.

night and day] Paul's usual order; 1 Thess. ii. 9, iii. 10; 1 Tim. v. 5; 2 Tim. i. 3. It has no connexion with the custom of counting days from evening to morning. 'Day and night' is frequent in both O.T. and N.T. The missionaries worked hard, and often worked at night. This is the contrast to 'without earning it,' ἐργαζόμενοι as opposed to δωρεάν.

9. **not because we have no right**] The ellipse, whether in English or in Greek (οὐχ ὅτι) is very intelligible; 'I do not say this because,' or 'I do not mean that.' Vulg. has *non quasi*, which would require οὐχ ὡς: *non quia* (Aug.) is right. Their working hard was not meant as a protest against the principle that ministers have a claim to maintenance; that principle is just; 1 Cor. ix. 3–14; 1 Tim. v. 18. But ministers are not bound to press that claim; and St. Paul habitually protested against its being made in favour of himself. It was a right which he declined to use. 'Right' is a late meaning of ἐξουσία, which originally meant 'freedom to act.' When this freedom was confirmed by law it became "authority" or 'right'; *e.g.* 'In virtue of what kind of "authority," of what kind of right, doest thou these things?' Mk. xi. 28 and parallels. The A.V. here has 'power' instead of 'right,' following *potestatem* in the Vulgate. See Robertson and Plummer on 1 Cor. ix. 4, 14. The Didache (xiii. 1) says that "every genuine prophet is worthy of his maintenance." *

Apparently the waiving of the right had given an opening to the enemy. They said that he did not dare to claim maintenance, because he knew that he was not really an Apostle. So he states what the true reason for refusing maintenance was.

but we did it in order to] The Greek is again elliptical: it gives simply 'but in order to,' ἀλλ' ἵνα. We may supply either 'we did it,' or 'we waived this right.' The former is simpler, but 1 Cor. ix. 15 rather favours the latter. See notes on the somewhat similar ellipse in ii. 3 and 7.

* It gives explicit directions about maintenance; "let every one that comes in the Name of the Lord be received, and then by testing him ye shall know. . . . If he wishes to settle among you, being a craftsman, let him work and eat. But if he has no handicraft, provide according to your common sense that no Christian shall live with idleness. But if he refuses (οὐ θέλει) to act thus, he is a Christ-monger (χριστέμπερος, making gain out of his Christian profession). Beware of such people" (xii. 1–5). Cf. Ignatius, *Eph.* vii. 1.

to give ourselves to you as an example] Both A.V. and R.V. have 'make ourselves an ensample'; but it is better to retain 'give' (δῶμεν). There was *self-sacrifice* in setting this example of working to maintain themselves, when they might justly have claimed maintenance. Cf. 1 Thess. ii. 8. As in 1 Thess. i. 7 we have τύπον, not τύπους. It was the missionaries collectively that gave the example. The metaphor is taken from sculpture; a τύπος is a model roughly chipped out; Rom. v. 14; Phil. iii. 17; 1 Tim. iv. 12; Tit. ii. 7. Thus there are here two reasons why the Apostle and his colleagues worked at a handicraft; to save their converts from expense, and to set a good example. There was also a third; to have something to bestow on others (Acts xx. 34). "The new religion did not teach 'the dignity of labour.' What it inculcated was just the *duty* of work" (Harnack, *Expansion*, I. pp. 173–5). 'Ourselves' (ἑαυτούς) is placed first with emphasis.

imitate us] The A.V. again has the inadequate 'follow us.' It was a pattern for them to copy that was given.

10. **And besides**] The conjunctions (καὶ γάρ) introduce an additional reason, as in 1 Thess. iii. 4, iv. 10; 1 Cor. v. 7, viii. 5, etc. The first reason is in *v.* 7.

when we were with you] See on ii. 5; πρός with the acc. after a verb of rest is the dominant use in N.T.; ii. 5; 1 Thess. iii. 4; Gal. iv. 18, 20; etc.

we repeatedly gave you] Imperfect tense, παρηγγέλλομεν. Evidently there were loafers among the first converts.

to this effect] 'This' is emphatic by position, as in 1 Thess. iv. 3.

does not choose to work] 'Would not work' (R.V.) is not quite so forcible as οὐ θέλει ἐργάζεσθαι, which implies refusal; cf. οὐχ ὑπακούει, *v.* 14. As Bengel points out, unwillingness in such a case is a vice, *nolle vitium est.* In each place the negative is part of the verb, 'is unwilling,' 'is disobedient'; hence οὐ, not μή, which would mean 'unless.' Burton, *Moods and Tenses*, § 469. See on 1 Cor. vii. 9.

neither let him eat] The Jews recognized this principle, deducing it from Gen. iii. 19, 'In the sweat of thy face shalt thou eat bread.' "Let not him who would not labour before the Sabbath eat on the Sabbath." Cf. Eccles. i. 13, iii. 10, 'travail that God hath given to the sons of men to be exercised therewith.' Wetstein quotes Rabbinical passages, but they belong to the fourth century, and they may be derived from this Epistle, and they do not declare so clearly as the Apostle does the moral obligation to work. See Deissmann, *Light from the Anc. East*, pp. 317 f. As Hesiod says, *Ἔργον δ' οὐδὲν ὄνειδος, ἀεργίη δὲ τ' ὄνειδος*, and Thales, *Ἀργὸς μὴ ἴσθι, μηδ' ἂν πλουτῇς.* This apostolic principle (which is often quoted by Jerome and by Cassian) indicates that inherited wealth does not absolve a man from the duty of work. Wealth is a trust, and to administer it rightly involves much thought and labour. Calvin uses the charge as a stone to throw at monks, *qui nihil agendo large saginantur; nisi qui taedii fallandi causa in templis cantillant.*

With *μηδὲ ἐσθιέτω* (strong negative) cf. *μηδὲ ὀνομαζέσθω* Eph. v. 3. The Vulg. has *nec* in both places; *ne quidem* would be better. Note the change from *οὐ* of the fact to *μηδέ* of the charge; also *ὅτι* introducing an imperative, as in Jn. ix. 11. Simcox, *Language of the N.T.* pp. 117, 122. The present tenses imply persistence.

11. **for reports are reaching us**] See on *v.* 7. Since the First Epistle was written the missionaries have been hearing, probably by letter, about these unsatisfactory converts: it is now necessary to deal with them; cf. 1 Cor. xi. 18. The Vulg. inaccurately has *audivimus*, but Fuld. and Am. have *audimus.*

certain persons] 'That there are some which' (A.V., Vulg. *quosdam*) is not exact. The *τινας* (*ἀκούομεν γάρ τινας*) intimates that they are known to the writers, 'we hear of some that' (R.V.). For *τινες* used of persons known, but not named, see 1 Cor. iv. 18, xv. 12; 2 Cor. iii. 1, x. 2; Gal. i. 7; 1 Tim. i. 3, 19, etc.

leading among you disorderly lives] The same expression as in *v.* 6. 'Among you,' looks back to *v.* 7; 'when *we* were among you we did not behave in this way'; ἐν ὑμῖν in both places.

who work not at all at their own business, but are busily engaged in doing nothing] This is an attempt to reproduce a play upon words, such as St. Paul is fond of making, μηδὲν ἐργαζομένους ἀλλὰ περιεργαζομένους: 'Busybodies who do no business' (Conybeare and Howson), 'doing no business but being busybodies' (Ellicott), 'busy only with what is not their own business' (Jowett), 'minding everybody's business sooner than their own' (Rutherford), *nihil operantes, sed curiose agentes* (Vulg.), *nihil operis agentes, sed curiose satagentes* (Calvin). Lünemann quotes from Quintilian, *non agere dixit sed satagere.* Jowett quotes from Demosthenes, ἐργάζῃ καὶ περιεργάζῃ τοὺς ἐσχάτους ὄντας κινδύνους. Excepting Ecclus. iii. 23, περιεργάζεσθαι occurs nowhere else in Bibl. Grk.*

Other instances of play between a simple and a compound are φρονεῖν and ὑπερφρονεῖν Rom. xii. 3, χρώμενοι and καταχρώμενοι 1 Cor. vii. 31, λαμβάνει and καταλάβητε 1 Cor. ix. 24, 25, γινωσκομένη and ἀναγινωσκομένη 2 Cor. iii. 2, ἀπορούμενοι and ἐξαπορούμενοι 2 Cor. iv. 8, ἔχοντες and κατέχοντες 2 Cor. vi. 10. Also between two compounds, ἀναγινώσκετε and ἐπιγινώσχετε 2 Cor. i. 13, ἐνκρῖναι and συνκρῖναι 2 Cor. x. 12, κατατομή and περιτομή Phil. iii. 3; and there are other variations.

12. **Now it is people of this kind]** Cf. Rom. xvi. 18; 1 Cor. v. 11; 2 Cor. xi. 13; Phil. ii. 29. In. *v.* 6 the well-conducted majority are told how to treat the offenders; here the offenders themselves are addressed, the περίεργοι (1 Tim. v. 13).

we command and exhort] The alliteration of παραγγέλλομεν καὶ παρακαλοῦμεν cannot be reproduced in English without spoiling the meaning, for here the second verb does not mean 'console' or 'comfort.' 'Counsel' perhaps might serve,

* Gregory Nazianzen (*Orat.* xxvi.) says, "I would rather be an unduly idle body than a busybody" (ἀργὸς ἢ περιέργος). Plato (*Rep.*, IV. 433 A) defines Justice as τὸ τὰ ἑαυτοῦ πράττειν καὶ μὴ πολυπραγμονεῖν.

but 'exhort' (A.V., R.V.) is better. 'Exhort' may be added in order to soften the sternness of 'command.' See on 1 Thess. iv. 1, where, as here, 'in the Lord Jesus' is added to 'exhort,' meaning 'in His Name,' as His ambassadors. 'By our Lord Jesus Christ' (A.V.) is based on an inferior reading, *διὰ τοῦ Κ. ἡμῶν Ἰ. Χρ.*

with quietness] This is the opposite of being busybodies. It implies freedom from internal excitement and external fussiness; 1 Thess. iv. 11; 1 Tim. ii. 11, 12; Ecclus. xxviii. 16. They are to be sober and cease from meddling. Vulg. has *cum silentio*: *cum tranquillitate* would be better.

the bread which they have earned] Literally, 'their own bread,' *τὸν ἑαυτῶν ἄρτον*, not that which others have earned, and which the idlers get for nothing; Cf. *τὰ ἀλλότρια δείπνειν*, *cibus alienus*, and *Ut bona summa putes aliena vivere quadra*, Juv. v. 2. "It needs to be proclaimed aloud that for the idle man there is no place in this England of ours. He that will not work, and save according to his means, let him go elsewhither; let him know that by the Law of Nature he is doomed either to quit these habits, or miserably be extruded from this Earth, which is made on principles different from these" (Carlyle, *Chartism*, ch. iii.).

13–15. *Instruction to the Loyal.*

[13] But ye, brethren, be not weary in well doing. [14] And if any man obey not our word, by this Epistle note that man, and have no company with him, that he may be ashamed, [15] Yet count him not as an enemy, but admonish him as a brother.

These directions, like those in *vv.* 6–10, are worthy of the Apostle, alike in their wisdom, their firmness, and their tenderness. It is difficult to attribute so apostolic a spirit to a mere imitator. "One of our greatest temptations is not to rebuke at all. No authority from St. Paul can be quoted for such a treatment either of sin or of the sinner. He is far too conscious of the destructiveness of sin and of its infectiousness" (Chadwick, *Pastoral Teaching of St. Paul*, p. 237; see also pp. 319, 321).

[13] But with regard to all you who are not offending in this way we exhort you, Brethren, not to falter in your noble course. [14] But, in order to maintain it, if any one is refusing to obey the charge which we have given in our letter, set a mark on this person, to the effect that you are not in any way to associate with him, that he may be put to shame. [15] And of course do this in a loving spirit. Do not in any way regard him as an enemy, but admonish him as a brother.

13. **But with regard to all you**] From the rebuke to the disorderly the writers return to the instructions which they have to give to the sober-minded majority. In some cases the rebuke may fail, and the loyal majority must know how to deal with such misbehaviour. The contrast between the loyal and the others is marked by an emphatic pronoun and an expressive particle, Ὑμεῖς δέ. See on 1 Thess. v. 4, where we have a similar transition; also Jude 17, 20.

not to falter] Not to take refuge in feeble inactivity. The verb (ἐγκάκειν) indicates the timidity which shrinks from speaking out and risking criticism and opposition. In Eph. iii. 13 μὴ εγκακεῖν follows a mention of 'boldness' (παρρησία) of which this faltering is the opposite. Excepting Lk. xviii. 1, the verb in N.T. is exclusively Pauline; 2 Cor. iv. 1, 16; Gal. vi. 9. 'Be not weary' (A.V., R.V.) misses the point both here and Gal. vi. 9. See on Lk. xviii. 1 and 2 Cor. iv. 1. In all six places ἐκκακ. occurs as a various reading. The verb is not found in LXX.

in your noble course] 'In well-doing' is perhaps too indefinite. 'Well-doing' implies general good conduct and benevolence in particular. And indeed Chrysostom, Theodoret, Calvin and Ewald interpret it of charitable action; as if it meant 'Do not abstain from being benevolent because unworthy people have abused your benevolence.' As Lightfoot points out, this restricted meaning would be possible with ἀγαθοποιεῖν, but not with καλοποιεῖν, which occurs nowhere else in Bibl. Grk. We have τὸ καλὸν ποιεῖν Rom. vii. 21; 2 Cor. xiii. 7; Gal. vi. 9; and ἀγαθοποιεῖν Mk. iii. 4; Lk. vi. 33, 35.

There may here be another play upon words, for μὴ ἐγκακήσητε καλοποιοῦντες suggests the opposition between *κακός* and *καλός*, between what is cowardly and what is noble and brave.

14. **But**] Seeing that the Thessalonians had been warned about this evil (1 Thess. iv. 11, v. 13, 14), and that it had evidently increased, therefore, so far from letting things slide and shirking unpleasantness, the loyal majority must be firm. 'Do not falter, but be strict.'

the charge which we have given in our letter] Doubtless this is the right connexion; 'in' or 'through our letter' belongs to what precedes, and *τῷ λόγῳ ἡμῶν διὰ τῆς ἐπιστολῆς* is all one phrase, meaning 'our word as sent in the letter which we are writing,' *nostro per epistolam sermoni* (Beza). The article (*τῆς*), as often, is equivalent to a possessive pronoun. Cf. *τὴν ἐπιστολήν* 1 Thess. v. 27 and Rom. xvi. 22, *ἡ ἐπιστολή* Col. iv. 16; also *τὴν συναγωγήν* Lk. vii. 5.

set a mark on this person] Some commentators connect 'through the letter' with this command; 'By means of the letter brand him as an offender.' Assuming this to be correct, it may be understood in two ways; either 'Use *this* letter for the purpose of convicting him,' or 'By means of *your* letter to *us* report him as a marked man.' Both of these interpretations are objectionable, because they lay an emphasis on the letter which is unnatural; the important point is that a rebel of this kind is to be noted and disgraced. The second interpretation is open to the further objection that it assumes that the loyal Thessalonians are to write back to the Apostle, about which no hint is given elsewhere. If this were meant, it would be more clearly expressed. Moreover, how improbable it is that there was to be a letter to Corinth and a letter back to Thessalonica before the matter was settled! The proposed connexion is wrong; 'our word conveyed through this letter' is the true connexion. The Thessalonians had the injunction in black and white, and that sufficed. How the mark is to be set on the rebellious person is not specified; probably by censure in the congregation.

not in any way to associate with him] Literally, 'not to mix yourselves up together with him,' *μὴ συναναμίγνυσθαι* αὐτῷ. The double compound expresses combination (σύν) and interchange (ἀνά). It occurs in a similar connexion 1 Cor. v. 9, 11, and in the A text of Ezek. xx. 18 and Hos. vii. 8. Here again the method is not specified. Intimacy is prohibited; intercourse for remonstrance (which Chrysostom thinks was to be in private) is enjoined. Calvin remarks that contumacy is worse than disorderly behaviour, and therefore excommunication must be meant. He adds that the object of excommunication is not alienation but recovery.

that he may be put to shame] The object is remedial, not vindictive. Pressure must be put upon the rebel to induce him to cease to be a scandal to the Church. The verb ἐντρέπειν occurs in the same sense 1 Cor. iv. 14 and 2 Chron. xii. 7; cf. ἐντροπή 1 Cor. vi. 5, xv. 34. The root-meaning is uncertain; perhaps to make a person 'hang his head' as a sign either of reverence (Tit. ii. 8 and Heb. xii. 9) or of shame (Ps. xxxiv. 4, lxix. 2).

15. **And**] We might have expected 'But,' ἀλλά rather than καί. The A.V. has 'Yet,' and the R.V. 'And *yet*,' the italics showing that 'yet' is not in the Greek. 'Yet' is neither expressed nor implied. There is no contrast, but a continuation of the kindly intent. It is assumed that the man will be ashamed and will repent; so of course he must be treated gently. The writers, while insisting on firmness, make clear that there must be no needless severity; so soon as the prescribed remedy has had the desired effect severity must cease.

as an enemy] This might be fatal, provoking the man to be still more obstinate in resisting. The Didache (xv. 3) again has a similar injunction; "Reprove one another, not in wrath, but in peace, as ye have it in the Gospel." Polycarp (xi. 4) reproduces the Apostle's words: "Hold not such as enemies, but restore them as frail and erring members, that you may save the whole body of you." Cf. Job xix. 11 ἡγήσατο δέ με ὡς ἐχθρόν.

admonish] Literally, 'put in mind' (νουθετεῖτε), but always of putting a person in mind of his duty, calling attention to failings, 1 Thess. v. 14; Rom. xv. 14; 1 Cor. iv. 14; Col. i. 28, iii. 16. The only other place in which the verb occurs in N.T. is in St. Paul's speech at Miletus, Acts xx. 31. Cf. Job. iv. 3; Wisd. xi. 11, xii. 2, 26; and **νουθεσία** Tit. iii. 10. See Trench, *Syn.*, § xxxii.; Cremer, *Lexicon*, p. 441. The Apostle's instructions in 2 Cor. ii. 6, 7 respecting the great offender, who is certainly not to be identified with the incestuous person in 1 Cor. v., should be compared. Our Lord's instructions (Mt. xviii. 15–17) are not quite parallel. They can be transferred to Christians, but they were addressed to Jews, and the **ἐκκλησία** or 'Assembly' means a Jewish Assembly, and probably the local synagogue. In all these instances, if the offender yields, he is to be forgiven and restored.

16. Prayer for the Thessalonians

16 Now the Lord of peace himself give peace always, by all means. The Lord be with you all.

The letter draws rapidly to a close. Like the first and second main divisions of it, the third division ends with a prayer for the converts; i. 11, 12–ii. 16, 17–iii. 16.

16 But enough of this subject. May the Lord who is the Prince of Peace Himself give you the peace that is His through all vicissitudes and in all ways. May the Lord be with you all.

16. **But]** In two ways there is something of contrast with what precedes. The writers turn with relief from the duty of enforcing discipline to that of intercession; and there is the thought that discipline will be useless unless it is blessed by the Lord. See above on ii. 16, where, as here, the transition is made by **Αὐτός δέ**.

the Lord] Here, as in *v.* 1, the question is raised whether 'the Lord' means Christ or the Father, and in both places it is safer to hold to Pauline usage and interpret it as meaning Christ. Thus, as in ii. 16, we have a prayer directed to Christ. In 1 Thess. v. 23, which is parallel to this verse, we have **Αὐτὸς δὲ ὁ Θεὸς τῆς εἰρήνης**: see the notes there and also on 1 Thess. iii. 11. 'The *God* of peace' is a frequent expression; Rom. xv. 33, xvi. 20; Phil. iv. 9; cf. 1 Cor xiv. 33; 2 Cor. xiii. 11; Heb. xiii. 20; Testaments, *Dan.* v. 2. 'The *Lord* of peace' occurs nowhere else, and some Latin authorities have *Deus* here, probably from 1 Thess. v. 23. We may suppose that the difference of expression indicates a difference of meaning. Here peace from unhealthy excitement and consequent dissension is chiefly meant. See Rostron, *Christology of St. Paul*, p. 48.

give] Note δῴη, the true optative, as in Rom. xv. 5, and 2 Tim. i. 16, 18; not δώῃ, which would be the subjunctive, as in Eph. i. 17: δῴη is a late form of δοίη. A. T. Robertson, *Grammar*, p. 938; Moulton, p. 194; Burton, § 175–177.

through all vicissitudes] The exact meaning of διὰ παντός is uncertain, but neither 'always' (A.V.) nor 'at all times' (R.V.) seems to be right. 'Always' would be ἀεί, which St. Paul rarely uses (2 Cor. iv. 11, vi. 10), and 'at all times' would be πάντοτε, which is very frequent (see note on πάντοτε i. 3). A.V. and R.V. have 'alway' for διὰ παντός in Acts x. 2, and 'continually' in Heb. xiii. 15: in Heb. ix. 6 A.V. has 'always,' and R.V. 'continually.' Why not 'continually' in all places? While πάντοτε points to every separate occasion, διὰ παντός points to a continual habit, without break. The latter is what is prayed for here. Whatever happens, may there be no break in the flow of Christ's peace,—τὴν εἰρήνην, the peace which it is specially His to give, Jn. xiv. 27, xvi. 33; Col. iii. 15.

in all ways] 'Whatever may befall you.' Weymouth suggests 'in every sense.' We may safely adopt τρόπῳ rather than τόπῳ as the original reading; cf. ii. 3; Phil. i. 18; Rom. iii. 2. When διὰ παντός is interpreted to mean 'at every time,' then it is natural to have ἐν παντὶ τόπῳ to follow; 'at every time and every place.' Moreover ἐν παντὶ τόπῳ occurs 1 Thess. i. 8; 1 Cor. i. 2; 2 Cor. ii. 14; 1 Tim. ii. 8. Copyists would be likely to change the less easy and less usual phrase into the more easy and more familiar one.

The Lord be with you all] The Lord who is Himself our peace, Eph. ii. 14. 'All' is exceptional in these concluding benedictions, but we have it 1 Cor. xvi. 24 and 2 Cor. xiii. 13. In all these three Epistles St. Paul has had to say some severe things respecting unsatisfactory members of the community: but none are excluded from the sweep of the Apostle's prayer for their spiritual progress and perfection. The final benediction in 1 Pet. v. 14 has 'peace' instead of the usual 'grace,' and also has 'all,' as here. See Bigg *ad loc.* Cf. Judg. vi. 12; Ruth ii. 4.

iii. 17, 18. CONCLUDING SALUTATION AND BENEDICTION

17 The salutation of Paul, with mine own hand, which is the token in every Epistle: so I write. 18 The grace of our Lord Jesus Christ *be* with you all, Amen.

In the Epistles these concluding words take the place of the conventional 'Fare ye well' (ἔρρωσθε, Acts xv. 29) in ordinary correspondence.

17 I, Paul, add the salutation with my own hand, and my doing so is a token by which every letter that comes from me may be known. This is my own handwriting. 18 The grace of our Lord Jesus Christ be with you all.

17. **the salutation with my own hand**] 'The salutation' which is usual. The statement that it is written with his own hand is added 1 Cor. xvi. 21 and Col. iv. 18, as also is the name Paul,—*τῇ ἐμῇ χειρὶ Παύλου*, the name being in the genitive in agreement with ἐμῇ, which is equivalent to a genitive. A. T. Robertson, *Grammar*, p. 493. Silvanus and Timothy are not included here; nor is Sosthenes or Timothy in the other cases. Writing the salutation *with his own hand* is the token. Some take the insertion of these words to be the token; but that cannot be correct, as the words are found only in 1 Corinthians and Colossians.

a token] A sign (σημεῖον) of the genuineness of the Epistle, that it really comes from the Apostle Paul. Gal. vi. 11

tells us that he wrote in large characters, which could easily be read and recognized as his. He dictated his letters (Rom. xvi. 22). But near the end he added something in his own handwriting,—always the concluding Salutation, and sometimes a little more. In Galatians the last eight verses were written by himself; and it is probable that the whole of the private letters to Philemon (*v.* 19) was written by himself. The four cases in which he mentions the fact that he is writing with his own hand are certainly not the only cases in which he does so. His reason for doing so in this place is that he thought it possible that a letter had been forged; see on ii. 2. In the other three cases we do not know his motive, but no doubt he had one. We cannot be sure that the concluding words of 1 Thessalonians were written by the Apostle himself. It may be that the idea did not occur to him until he found that he and his colleagues were being quoted as having said what they had not said.*

Deissmann (*Light*, p. 153) remarks that "the hundreds of autograph signatures to papyrus letters are greatly in need of investigation. A study of them would lead to a better appreciation of that extremely important passage in 2 Thess. iii. 17, which some most strangely regard as a mark of spuriousness." See also p. 158.

This is my handwriting] This seems to be the meaning of 'So I write,' *οὕτως γράφω*. In Gal. vi. 11 he calls attention to the size of his handwriting. Rutherford translates, 'Mark the handwriting.' If this is correct, it almost implies that the conclusion of 1 Thessalonians was written by himself. It seems to imply that the recipients would know the look of his handwriting, and if any one questioned the authenticity of 2 Thessalonians, they would show him the two conclusions as being evidently in the same hand. In any case, this precaution comes more naturally in a second letter than in a first, and is against the theory, now perhaps extinct, that 2 Thess. was written before 1 Thess.

* Cicero writes to Atticus (VIII. i. 1). *In ea Pompeii epistola erat in extremo, ipsius manu*: Tu, censeo, Luceriam venias, nusquam eris tutius

Some understand 'So I write' as meaning 'Writing the concluding salutation with my own hand is my habitual practice.' The words can hardly mean 'This is the formula, without which no letter is genuine.' Any imitator could adopt a formula; and such a meaning would be differently expressed. The suggestion that 'so I write' refers to some peculiar flourish is grotesque.

18. **The grace of our Lord**] See on 1 Thess. v. 28. The addition of 'all' is the only difference.

As in 1 Thess. and in most places in the N.T., the concluding 'Amen' is a later addition taken from the liturgies.

Indexes

INDEX I. GENERAL

INDEX II. GREEK

Printed in Great Britain for Robert Scott, *Publisher*, Paternoster Row, London, E.C.4.
by Butler & Tanner, Frome